Against Sex Education

Radical Politics and Education

Series editors: Derek R. Ford and Tyson E. Lewis

With movements against oppression and exploitation heightening across the globe, radical activists and researchers are increasingly turning to educational theory to understand the pedagogical aspects of struggle. The Radical Politics and Education series opens a space at this critical juncture, one that pushes past standard expositions of critical education and critical pedagogy. Recognizing the need to push political and educational formulations into new theoretical and practical terrains, the series is an opportunity for activists, political thinkers, and educational philosophers to cross disciplinary divides and meet in common. This kind of dialogue is crucially needed as political struggles are increasingly concerned with questions of how to educate themselves and others, and as educational philosophy attempts to redefine itself beyond academic norms and disciplinary values. This series serves to facilitate new conversations at and beyond these borders.

Advisory board:

Jodi Dean *(Hobart and William Smith Colleges, USA)*
Margret Grebowicz *(University of Silesia, Poland)*
Davide Panagia *(University of California, Los Angeles, USA)*
Patti Lather *(Ohio State University, USA)*
Nathan Snaza *(University of Richmond, USA)*
Stefano Harney *(Singapore Management University, Singapore)*

Also available in the series:

A History of Education for the Many: From Colonization and Slavery to the Decline of US Imperialism, Curry Malott

Experiments in Decolonizing the University: Towards an Ecology of Study, Hans Schildermans

Rethinking Philosophy for Children: Agamben and Education as Pure Means, Tyson E. Lewis and Igor Jasinski

Forthcoming in the series:

Education, Society, and the Philosophy of Louis Althusser, David I. Backer

Queers Teach This!: Queer and Trans Pleasures, Politics, and Pedagogues, Adam J. Greteman

A Voice for Maria Favela: An Adventure in Creative Literacy, Antonio Leal

Against Sex Education

Pedagogy, Sex Work, and State Violence

Caitlin Howlett

BLOOMSBURY ACADEMIC
LONDON • NEW YORK • OXFORD • NEW DELHI • SYDNEY

BLOOMSBURY ACADEMIC
Bloomsbury Publishing Plc
50 Bedford Square, London, WC1B 3DP, UK
1385 Broadway, New York, NY 10018, USA
29 Earlsfort Terrace, Dublin 2, Ireland

BLOOMSBURY, BLOOMSBURY ACADEMIC and the Diana logo are trademarks of
Bloomsbury Publishing Plc

First published in Great Britain 2022
This paperback edition published in 2023

Copyright © Caitlin Howlett, 2022

Caitlin Howlett has asserted her right under the Copyright, Designs and Patents Act, 1988,
to be identified as Author of this work.

For legal purposes the Acknowledgments on p. vi constitute an extension of
this copyright page.

Series design by Adriana Brioso
Cover image © bortonia/iStock

This work is published subject to a Creative Commons Attribution Non-commercial
No Derivatives Licence. You may share this work for non-commercial purposes only,
provided you give attribution to the copyright holder and the publisher.

Bloomsbury Publishing Plc does not have any control over, or responsibility for, any
third-party websites referred to or in this book. All internet addresses given in this
book were correct at the time of going to press. The author and publisher regret any
inconvenience caused if addresses have changed or sites have ceased to exist,
but can accept no responsibility for any such changes.

A catalogue record for this book is available from the British Library.

A catalogue record for this book is available from the Library of Congress

Library of Congress Cataloging-in-Publication Data

Names: Howlett, Caitlin, author.
Title: Against sex education: pedagogy, sex work, and state violence / Caitlin Howlett.
Description: London; New York: Bloomsbury Academic, 2021. |
Series: Radical politics and education | Includes bibliographical references and index. |
Identifiers: LCCN 2021013787 (print) | LCCN 2021013788 (ebook) |
ISBN 9781350178441 (hardback) | ISBN 9781350178458 (ebook) |
ISBN 9781350178465 (epub)
Subjects: LCSH: Sex instruction. | Sex workers. | Exploitation. |
Sexism. | Colonization.
Classification: LCC HQ56.H833 2021 (print) |
LCC HQ56 (ebook) | DDC 613.9071/2–dc23
LC record available at https://lccn.loc.gov/2021013787
LC ebook record available at https://lccn.loc.gov/2021013788

ISBN: HB: 978-1-3501-7844-1
PB: 978-1-3502-2506-0
ePDF: 978-1-3501-7845-8
eBook: 978-1-3501-7846-5

Series: Radical Politics and Education

Typeset by Deanta Global Publishing Services, Chennai, India

To find out more about our authors and books visit
www.bloomsbury.com and sign up for our newsletters.

Contents

Acknowledgments	vi
Introduction: Making Something Out of Nothing	1
1 Origin Problems	19
2 Small, but Mighty: A Little Funding for a Huge Cause	47
3 Violent Straightening and the Function of the State	69
4 The International Implications of Domestic Sex Education Policy	89
5 Alternatives, Not Adjustments; Imagination, Not Intervention	111
Conclusion: Clandestine Praxes	131
Notes	139
Bibliography	157
Index	165

Acknowledgments

Single authored books are scams; the good here exists only because of others. Kristen. Polly. Libba. Shed. Quentin. Sylvia. LaMonda. Luise. Barry. Marlon. Friday Group. Thanks for taking a chance on me, for keeping me both on my toes and in my lane, and for giving me thousands of pages of life-altering words to read.

My first attempt at writing this book coincided with my transition out of grad school and into DePauw University. Many DePauw faculty, across disciplines, spent a lot of time and energy generously talking me through the process in various writing groups and virtual get-togethers, even while we all grappled with the changes necessitated by Covid-19. My DePauw students, too, especially those who have taken sex education courses with me, have made vital contributions to my thinking about the subject and to my overall well-being. I feel nothing but gratitude for those of you who helped me in these ways.

Thank you to Derek Ford and Tyson Lewis, as well as Mark Richardson and Evangeline Stanford at Bloomsbury Academic. You each were so kind and patient with me and helped me do work that I could be proud of. I am also indebted to the anonymous reviewers who offered critical insight into things I could not see on my own and made me think harder, too.

I cannot emphasize what I am about to say enough: *there would also be no book if it were not for my therapist and psychiatrist*. Both forces of nature in your own right, you took me seriously in a moment when I most needed to be treated as such, all while letting me be unapologetically me. Everyone everywhere deserves the kind of mental health care that you provided me with.

For every issue I have with the nuclear family, for every way that heteronormativity makes me eye-rolly, it is kind of strange how much I love and like my family. Somehow, I got two parents and a younger sibling who I actually *respect* and *admire* as an "adult." Even during and after disaster, I somehow keep finding new reasons to feel this way. Thank you for all that, and also for being just as critical interlocutors about these ideas and arguments as any other colleague has been. Shantay you stay. And to all the people I love and who love me and yet maybe don't even know that I did this thing or maybe will never even try to read this: the space you held and continue to hold for me to be something beyond all this is so invaluable to me. Thank you. This includes, of course, my godchildren and part-time children. But also, and especially, George.

And thank you to those whom I do not know, but who have inspired me from beyond the screens and the airwaves and the pages, from the past and the future (and sometimes both at the same time), and in any and all forms. By being so passionately, unapologetically, and viscerally yourselves, and by bringing new ways of living and loving into existence, you made people like me, *and* not at all like me, possible.

Introduction

Making Something Out of Nothing

> *SWOP, at its most basic, is an anti-violence campaign. As a multi-state network of sex workers and advocates, we address locally and nationally the violence that sex workers experience because of their criminal status. Operating in one of the most prominently violent societies today, sex workers in America experience this phenomenon pointedly in the context of their criminal status. Yet, sex workers are seldom afforded protection or recourse from violent acts committed against them because of the precarious, often graft-ridden relationship between sex work and law enforcement. Society tolerates violence against sex workers because of the stigma and myths that surround prostitution. Only until these falsehoods are corrected and sex workers are legitimized will we be able to effectively prevent and minimize the structural and occupational challenges of sex work.*
>
> Sex Workers Outreach Project—US Mission Statement

Sex education depends upon stories; stories about where and when to have sex, about who can or should have sex and with whom, about the moral significance of sex, and about the many ways sex can quite literally make or break a life or a family or a community. Like all stories, those that are shared as part of becoming "sexually educated" are filled with characters—sometimes real, sometimes fictional—that depict what is to be gained and what is to be lost when embarking upon sexual relationships. Albeit for different reasons, sex education routinely explores the consequences of sexual behavior through the stories of the teenage mother-to-be or the could-be teenage mother or the person living with HIV/AIDs (who you most certainly do *not* want to become, right?) and the virtuous, virginal, happy, heterosexual person looking for *real* love (look at the beautiful life you *could* have!). It is no game of chance: the story of sex education is one of choice, and the task of taking it is to learn how to get you to choose *correctly*. However, most students in the United States know, in some sense, that this is *not* actually the game, though, and that this is not *the* story. There are tremendous absences playing roles in these stories, too. And, as so many have been exploring and unpacking for decades, these absences have stories themselves. In other words, they have stories about *the* story, and this book explores just a small part of one.

Any story of the founding of federally funded sex education in the United States includes, in some way, accounts of the following moments, and as such, there are absences here that ignite, for me, a curiosity about the stories within them. I thus include these stories to spark curiosity in others and to bring the reader into the fold of making sense of the absences, as I will argue that there are lessons that need to be explored, too.

(1) Prince Morrow and Social Hygiene—In 1907, in the *American Journal of Sociology*, emerging sex education expert Prince Morrow's work, "Prophylaxis of Social Disease," was published. Concerned with the spread of venereal diseases, he writes that it is "not simply a struggle against microbes, but a warfare, as well, against bad social conditions."[1] The health of the nation is at stake, and it is the prostitute that grounds the fear of its destruction. It is her "illegitimate sexual relations" that cause the spread of diseases and that threaten the American family and the logics that maintain it.[2] At stake are the lives of those women who uphold the honor of the American family:

> It is upon women that the burden of shame and suffering of disease and death, is chiefly laid—not so much, perhaps upon that unfortunate class who are regarded as the chief agents in the propagation of the diseases, but upon pure women, who do not always find, even in the sanctuary of marriage, a safeguard against "the diseases of the women of the streets."[3]

In order for "general enlightenment" and "the safeguarding of marriage from venereal infections"[4] to be achieved, "efforts should be directed not to making prostitution safe, but to prevent the making of prostitutes."[5] Sex education is seen as a promising site for intervention into this family- and nation-destroying problem.

(2) Raymond Fosdick and Training Camp Activities—With the decision to enter the First World War came the establishment of soldier training camps within the United States, and, with that, the proliferation of

venereal disease at such an alarming rate near those camps that it was deemed a public health problem by the newly created Public Health Service.[6] This inspired the creation of the Commission of Training Camp Activities, made up of War and Navy Department branches, which was tasked with providing education about venereal disease. In 1918, the chairman of the War and Navy Departments, and newly appointed chairman of the Commission on Training Camp Activities, Raymond Fosdick expressed great personal concern for the threat posed by the infiltration of these diseases into the lives of soldiers. Referring to a camp in Columbus, New Mexico, he says of these soldiers that

> There was absolutely nothing in that town that could in any way legitimately interest them. There were no moving-picture shows and no pool tables; there was no place where they could write letters or read, no place where they could purchase a newspaper or magazine. The only attractions in town were a few disreputable saloons and a red-light district; and those institutions were extensively patronized because there was absolutely nothing to compete with them.[7]

The danger was great, but the solution was relatively simple: the federal government would fund the construction facilities such as libraries, theaters, athletic spaces, and meeting places (called "hostess houses") and more direct intervention into the "evil" that thrived in the "saloons" and "red-light districts" surrounding the camps.[8] Fosdick adds: "We are confronted with a special problem. These men are not enlisting voluntarily for service, but are being drafted, and we cannot afford to draft them into a demoralizing environment. They must be protected. It is a duty we that we own not only to the men themselves, but to their families when the men come back from overseas."[9] To this end, some of the first federally funded sex education materials and information were put into print.

(3) "Healthy Happy Womanhood"—In 1919, just a year after Fosdick expressed the necessity for sex education for soldiers, the US Public Health Service issued a "Pamphlet for Girls and Young Women" titled "Healthy Happy Womanhood" detailing a path for girls that, if followed, promises not just health and happiness but beauty, joy, popularity, and a husband and children to boot. This is the path *good, healthy* girls are to take: first, you must work on your physical fitness and "incidentally increase your beauty and attractiveness"; this good health also "produces

high spirits, vitality, cheerfulness and leadership," all of which will also make you popular.[10] Exercise, yes, but "always insist upon working in well-ventilated rooms," take cold baths, eat three meals and drink eight glasses of water every day, and do not forget to sleep: "A growing girl needs from 8 ½ to 9 ½ hours of sleep every night."[11] Take care of these things now so that you are ready for the moment when your body needs you most: motherhood. To this end, after this path toward wellness has been taken, the pamphlet offers anatomical and biological information about "glands and their functions," before moving on to an account of female reproductive organs and the process through which life begins. It describes, through a discussion of commonly known animals, the process of fertilization that occurs for many different species, and, like the animals, humans too, we are told, are driven by the "sex instinct," which "leads [animals and human beings] to create life and continue race."[12] Something that seems to make humans distinct, however, is "love"; "Love is due in a large measure to the sex instinct. All the fine emotions such as love of mother for child, of husband and wife, friendship, devotion to a great cause, and the joy which one finds in every day work are closely related to it."[13] A final note: "The sex instinct is a tremendous power in life. Used rightly it will bring to the individual and to the race the greatest joy; used wrongly it will not only fail to produce this result, but also it will probably lead to serious suffering and unhappiness." What might cause this suffering and unhappiness? We are told that it is "Sex relations among persons who are not married to each other,"[14] and that this suffering and unhappiness will also likely include a battle with syphilis, gonorrhea, or other venereal diseases. We learn, too, that it is women's responsibility to make sure she is not seen as an "easy mark" or that she does not "put herself in a position where a man can take advantage of her."[15] Indeed, take these precautions, and anything is possible: "To-day the opportunities for woman's development and her ability to contribute toward the creation of a better world are greater than ever before. At last all activities of life are open to her."[16] *This* is the role girls and young woman can play in working toward the "achievement" of national glory.

What stories are being produced and told in these instantiations of sex education's history, and how do we understand the importance of these stories? We could explore these moments in so many different ways, after all. For instance, we could talk about the men being inflicted with venereal disease or the men turning to sex education to help them. There are the people named themselves: Morrow, Fosdick, those at the US Public Health Service who crafted either the literature for the soldiers or the literature for the students. Or, we could center and highlight the experiences of the girls and women discussed, instead. Here, we would have to choose from within that group: the schoolgirls, or the healthy and dedicated wife? Or the prostitute? Yes, let's go with her.

Finding a Purpose

For me, it is the everlasting presence of the prostitute, or the sex worker, that I desperately wanted to know more about.[17] In my experience, being a student of education, so to speak, has meant either never acknowledging the existence of sex work or sex workers or, at the most, understanding their existence as valued only for the terrible lessons they have for those who dare stray from the well-trodden trail toward sexual conformity. Being of a certain class (middle-ish?), of a certain race (white), of a certain assigned gender and sex that I do indeed inhabit without significant tension or sacrifice ("woman"), and being sexually normative enough to avoid questioning, I was taught, albeit mostly implicitly, that the worst-case scenario for my own life was that I end up being "forced" into sex work. At the same time, I never cared much for the thing I was supposed to want, for the best-case scenario (the marriage, the kids, the house, etc.). If anything, I felt apathetic, and thus I primarily found sex education interesting in the abstract. Even as I decided that I most certainly did *not* want to be a high-school history teacher, three years into that undergraduate program, I continued to find it interesting as an academic pursuit until I did finally begin to find it *infuriating* as an academic pursuit that I *did* connect with at a personal level. The more I learned, the more annoyed I became, and I finally reached what I thought were peak-anger levels when I started to realize, in a tiny classroom in the building that used to house the Kinsey Institute with the help of many beloved others, that the worst-case scenario and the best-case scenario are essentially nothing without each other. There is no sex work without heteronormative marriage, and there is no heteronormative marriage without sex work. At the very least, *that* seems like a good enough reason to take a step back to ask the question of what the hell sex education is for.

My own situatedness and the historical moments shared above point me to a question about sex education that is often left out of much of the essential and innovative scholarship about how to make sex education *better*: Why does sex education exist? It seems like a simple question but, again, as I pondered the histories shared earlier, it quickly became clear that it is a far more complicated question to answer. I could make connections between these stories and contemporary concerns for diseases and pregnancy, yes, and in some ways, the "Healthy Happy Womanhood" pamphlet seems almost *better* than some of the material I was introduced to in my own sex education. But what about the other parts? What about the whole war part? Why in the world was a high-ranking member of what would become the *United States' defense department* taking up the eugenicist language of social hygiene to advocate for sex education? While we are at it, why was *that* language so similar to what showed up in these sex education pamphlets for girls? And prostitution? What about the prostitutes? I wanted to know more about who *they* were, what their presence in these spaces meant for sex education, and how that understanding might impact the issues with sex education that continue to plague the United States today.

There are already many important and powerful accounts of sex education's history, and many of them do offer explicit answers to the question of sex education's existence in meaningful ways. There remains, however, so much to be unpacked about sex education's past, especially as sex education in the present continues to flail in the face of ongoing sex-, gender-, sexuality-, and racist-related violence and the stakes for addressing this violence feel higher and higher. Despite the research that has been produced on sex education, and the many valuable ways it is seen as a site for such an intervention, there remains almost no evidence of widespread positive impacts of sex education, or even of more comprehensive sex education, in working toward a less-violent future. What we know more than anything else is that people *want* sex education that *better* reflects the needs and desires of today's world and thus can be part of progressive movements toward equity, recognition, and inclusion, but what we don't know is how to turn the former into something that can produce the latter. So, it remains an open question as to what has been misinterpreted along the way regarding sex education's purpose and efficacy. This project attempts to explore this misinterpretation by offering an alternative story about sex education by centering the very person who remains, at best, at the margins of discourses around sex education policy: the sex worker.

For what purposes *did* sex education come into existence as a federally funded program in the first place? This is a historiographical question, at least in part, as the "search for 'origins,'" as Foucault reminds us, is simultaneously a fantastical if not delusional task as well as a moralizing and normalizing one.[18] A historical approach that asserts its narrative as truth and as complete is one that makes a metaphysical claim about reality, resulting only in the creation of an illusion of coherence that masks the discrepancies and inconsistencies that are innate to all stories. The task of understanding is framed by "problematization," or what philosopher Colin Koopman describes as a task that "exposes us" to the central myths by which our experiences are normatively structured.[19] For example, Foucault writes that exploring the history of any contemporary event requires an openness to "'something altogether different' behind things: not a timeless and essential secret, but the secret that they have no essence or that their essence was fabricated in a piecemeal fashion in alien forms."[20] In exploring the so-called purpose of sex education, then, I am more interested in the stories that are told about it, and the ones that are *not*, than finding the "real" one. It is from this perspective that I endeavor to seek out answers to my questions about both the presence of the "prostitute"[21] and the purposes of sex education.

There are at least three dominant or prevailing discourses circulating the field of sex education regarding the beginning of federal involvement in the sexual education of US citizens and residents, each of which appears in some way in the moments discussed earlier: (1) public health and hygiene; (2) the regulation of female sexuality and sex difference; and (3) eugenics and the often explicit desire for the preservation of the white race. Though not entirely independent from each other, the prevalence of these three trends throughout this literature is telling not merely because of the understandings of sex education they perpetuate but because of the impact of this perpetuation on whose experiences are deemed most reliable and valuable in dissecting sex education's continued existence and possible worth today.

First, then, there is little disagreement that the most prevalent discourse regarding sex education's emergent existence as a subject of federal interest at the turn of the twentieth century in the United States among historians is one regarding public health and the concept of "hygiene." Alexandra Lord's powerful *Condom Nation*, for example, traces the history of the creation and increased centralization of sex education in America in a way that culminates in the argument that sex education is best understood as representing an instance of "the active intervention of the state in protecting its citizens' health has been central to American history."[22] Noting that while initial, informal sex education programs were popular with the American citizenry prior to the 1900s, she argues that contemporary discourses around morality, religion, and race coalesced into a particular sense of public health that then shaped how that public health was to be achieved. This moment was met with many voices, each eager to intervene upon the declining health of the United States and its citizens. Not the least of which was the newly defined "expert" of "science." Highlighted earlier, Prince A. Morrow is so often, and rightly I think, identified as a leading "expert" in shaping sex education's existence by using science to link public hygiene to sexual behavior. Morrow, a founding member of what would become the American Federation for Sex Hygiene, a predecessor of the American Social Hygiene Association, and prominent sex education researcher and proponent of the early 1900s, focused on particular forms of sexual deviancy as dirtying the health of the population. Most notable, as both Lord and Jeffery Moran in his book *Teaching Sex* argue, was his concern with the spread of venereal disease through prostitution. Moran brilliantly outlines how the social hygiene movement, spearheaded by Morrow, moved the perceived source of the problem of prostitution and disease from the individual to society as a whole. Moran writes that Morrow helped define these trends as "metaphors for social decline," affecting the most innocent and respectable members of society: married white women and their children.[23] Likewise, Huber and Firmin describe the emergence of sex education policies as explicitly bound to Morrow's work in linking immorality and sexual deviance under the guise of expertise. They write in their own account of sex education's history that the increased reliance upon newly developed medical and scientific language and knowledge was utilized by social hygienists, like Morrow, to simultaneously justify the need for formal intervention into the sexual behavior of those living within the US borders while provoking fear toward those who strayed from the ideal the intervention invoked.[24]

In an effort to explore the importance of the hygiene discourse, the Comstock Act of 1873 is almost always highlighted in these stories, too. That is, with the Comstock Act, which criminalized the selling and distribution of "obscene" material, as well as its transportation across state lines, all discussions of sex and sexuality were scrutinized for their possible obscenity. This requirement, even for conversation about sex, narrowly limited what could be proposed and even discussed in relation to sex education programs. Lord notes, "The Act cast a long shadow and sparked fear among not only pornographers, prostitutes, and others in the sex trade but also among those who promoted sex education or the use of contraceptives."[25] On her account, part of the possibility of public health, then, was understood in part as contingent upon the narrowing of sex's presence in the public sphere, and early consideration on the part of the federal government for sex education reflected this trend. Further, the generalized desire for public health is also connected to the prevalence of venereal disease that resulted during the First World War. For Lord, sex education thus served a specific function as a federal project: "By the early twentieth century, substantial precedents existed that allowed the federal government to draw upon its diverse powers to force the issue of sexually transmitted diseases into the open, to push sex education into the schools and the workplace, and to conduct research into the causes of and treatment for sexually transmitted diseases."[26] Situating the "origin" story of sex education within a discourse about public health therefore mirrors the legitimacy assumed by experts at the time regarding the purposes for which sex education was necessary.

Second, and intrinsic to the public health narrative, is the connection between sex education and the regulation of female sexuality and sex difference. A point of contentious debate within the Progressive era, the strengthening of the link between the white race, the traditional family, and the need to control, even criminalize, female sexuality, particularly as it was distinguished from the so-called nature of the male sex, is cited within sex education history as a founding motivation for its existence. Again, Lord centers this cause in her articulation of the impact of what was perceived by many in the upper classes as the destabilization of the American family, particularly due to industrialization, urbanization, and immigration. For Lord, the loosening of women's roles in the home caused by these societal shifts was itself a contributing factor in the public health crisis, and thus the emergence of federal interest in something to be called sex education is best understood as an antidote to the consequences of these shifts. According to

Jeffery Moran, people like Morrow also perpetuated the link between public health and female sexuality by linking the spread of disease to a particular expression of female sexuality: prostitution. He writes that this was "only one particular instance of the much broader concern at the turn of the century with defending women, the family, and, in many reformers' eyes, the race."[27] Further, Moran highlights the ways in which G. Stanley Hall came to the foreground in debates around public health by proposing the category of the "adolescent," a new category able to do the work of identifying and describing normal sexual behavior and development and thus solidifying the legitimacy of the "innocent" female. One of Moran's penultimate arguments about sex education as a federally funded project is that "the turn toward youth and the schools embodied a number of historically contingent factors, including the rise of expertise as a force in America culture, Prince Morrow's ideological disdain for coercion, and the ascendant Progressive faith in education."[28] Of course, the link between public health and sexuality that was developed at the time is often attributed to the tidal wave of expert literature on sexuality itself. Moran and Jonathan Zimmerman, author of *Too Hot to Handle: A Global History of Sex Education*, especially emphasize that it was people like Hall and also Freud who established a discourse that participated in the very kind of normalizing of control over female sexuality that made sex education a desirable endeavor.

The last prevailing thread that must be addressed is centered on race. That is, eugenics and the desire to preserve the superiority of the white American individual and family is always offered as an essential framework for understanding the purpose of sex education during the Progressive era. Lord writes convincingly about how the general anxiety around the influx non-"native" people into the United States was itself a reflection of the already festering, if not widely rampant, racist fear of nonwhite people. Citing the lingering effects of Jim Crow laws, for example, Lord details the way that such laws "fed into the widespread belief that nonwhites corrupted whites."[29] The oft discussed Mann Act of 1910, which aimed at preventing "white slavery," is particularly valuable evidence of this belief for historians of sex education. The threat to female sexuality caused by the decline of moral and physical wellness of the time was envisaged anew in the promotion of the fear around the possibility of young, innocent white women being held captive for the purposes of sex. It was therefore argued that sex education could also serve the purpose of spreading the word of this threat; it could give a voice to the victims of "white slavery" and ensure that the traditional, Victorian-style family and sexual ideals were protected and preserved for years to come. Notably, as Darlene Clark Hine, Dorothy Roberts, and many others have powerfully demonstrated, the very idea of reproductive freedom that was developed during this time was guided by a racist concern for the preservation of the white race. It is for this reason that almost all historians of sex education see Margaret Sanger's role in sex education's founding as important, as both her advocacy around birth control for women and the connection between that advocacy and eugenicist beliefs complicates the idea that sex education was in any way a truly "progressive" step. Sanger's work in arguing for public acknowledgment and acceptance of sex as pleasurable in and of itself, and thus not merely for the sake of reproduction, was, on Sanger's own account, tied to the idea that "cultural progress for future generations was possible through selective breeding or discriminatory reproduction."[30] In *Sex Ed, Segregated*, for example, Courtney Q. Shah shows how "American racism complicated sex education" from the start and summarizes the main point of this narrative: sex education "could have been a revolutionary way of empowering people but instead was more often used to reinforce power relations."[31]

It is important to add here that there is at least one other essential umbrella concept related to understanding sex education's existence that is both connected to each of the above threads while also distinct enough, particularly giving this project's interest in education, to warrant brief attention: the Progressive-era faith in the potential of education, in general and in its publicly funded form, to solve social problems, especially those related to social "instability" and family life. For instance, Huber and Firmin cite the work of Ella Flagg Young as exemplary of the ways in which public health issues were increasingly seen as educational issues during the Progressive era. They write about how schools, for Young and many others, were perfect laboratories for experimenting on children to see how best to effectively combat unhealthy and immoral sexual behavior.[32] Similarly, Julian Carter's important examination of the intellectual history of sex education posits that this Progressive-era "confidence in education" led to "profound ambivalence" regarding its construction and institution.[33] Carter carefully explores the "logic of contagion" that surrounded sex education discourse during this era, and, as Robin Jensen argues later in her work, the rhetorical confusion produced in these discourses cultivated a uniquely Progressive-era ambiguity around sex education, such that it was difficult to even speak about.[34]

Taken together, then, these historiographical narratives exhibit the way historians of education have accounted for sex education's "origins" and can be seen as aligning with a view of sex education that situates the federal project of sex education as a Progressive public health initiative aimed at maintaining the social, cultural, political, and epistemological status of the traditional white American family through idealizations of femininity as pure, innocent, and in need of protection. As discussed earlier, however, my interest is in a specific set of questions about the lives centered in these histories and the assumptions, epistemological and normative, that such centering depends upon in order to be justifiable. In other words, here, I aim to problematize the stability of the threads just discussed or to refuse to take for granted the processes of humanization and dehumanization at play in them, always guided by my original question about the presence of sex workers within these narratives.

Biopolitics, Erasures, and Reorientation

Sex education, then, is explored here as a kind of biopolitical device. In its existence as a federal policy, it operates for the exclusive purpose of distinguishing between life and death in its many forms. To live is to be seen, to matter, to be spoken of, to be allowed to reproduce, to be rewarded, to be allowed to exist as an agent; to die is to be erased, to be in *need* of erasure, to be expelled, to be subhuman, to exist as a problem for other agents, to be allowed to die. In discussing the idea of biopolitics as it came into existence within modern discourses of sexuality, Foucault argues that the contrast between life and death is one that is upheld and negotiated through relations of power, language, and governance. Biopolitics, therefore, refers to a kind of political rationality, or a system of thought and practice "by which human behavior is directed via a state administration,"[35] that allows for and simultaneously justifies the enactment of differentiated forms of material and epistemological control across and between populations by way of laws, policies, and institutional norms. Foucault discusses such rationalities through a view of them *not* as "an absolute against which they could be evaluated as constituting more or less perfect forms of rationality" but instead as "inscriptions" that allow for biopolitical practices to be justifiably normalized.[36] So, biopolitics are those discursive practices that produce the logics and norms by which any part of a population is to be determined as worthy of life, and a certain kind of life at that.

In invoking this biopolitical framework, I explore how sex education participates in the construction and legitimization of biopolitical discourses, and therefore inquire into the ways that those logics are normalized via determinations about sexual normalcy and deviancy. In thinking about Foucault's notion of biopolitics, especially in relation to logics of sexual normalcy and deviance, I want to recall, too, a comment he makes elsewhere. He writes,

> Sexuality is a part of our behavior. It's a part of our world freedom. Sexuality is something that we ourselves create—it is our own creation, and much more than the discovery of a secret side of our desire. We have to understand that with our desires, through our desires, go new forms of relationships, new forms of love, new forms of creation. Sex is not a fatality; it's a possibility for creative life.[37]

When assessed alongside the concept of biopolitics, it becomes clear, I think, that, while yes, biopolitics is about life and death, it is also about *creation and reproduction*, too. This suggests something important about the stakes of understanding the biopolitical characteristics of sex education policies: sexuality is a site within which *possibility* itself is to be maintained, contained, and even restrained. If we desire something novel, or that rejects the violence inherent in federal sex education policies, or that something currently impossible becomes possible, the way that the creative impulse at the core of sexuality is itself erased in education must be accounted for, too.

To this point, L. H. Stallings offers an important critique and extension of Foucault's concern with power, knowledge, and sexuality, writing that, after Foucault, "we know what power does with sexuality and we understand the discourse of sex, but we understand less about what imagination does with sexuality and how imagination thwarts power's need to establish a knowledge-power of sex as either Scientia sexualis or a truth-as-pleasure from ars erotica."[38] My contention is, therefore, that sex education policies overwhelmingly erase, and thus produce, blind spots when it comes to sex workers, specifically by way of the circulation and perpetuation of a political rationality that itself normalizes their exclusion *and* makes the alternative, imaginative, and novel ways of living and loving and creating they enact seem both impossible *and* evil. Sex education limits what constitutes legitimate knowledge by explicitly refusing a specific understanding of sexuality—as art as experience.[39] So, the seeming impossibility of sex workers existing meaningfully in sex education policies is what makes it seem crazy to include them; their assumed inherent evil is what justifies their isolation from the child; and both their impossibility and evilness combined determine the distance from education itself at which they must be kept.

These are the distances I want to trouble and denaturalize and dismantle. It is imperative to understand sex workers first as actual, existing human beings and, second, as a legitimate source of knowledge about sex education's existence at the federal level. At the very least, we have enough information and understanding to ask about other ways of orienting and staging questions of sex education's purpose beyond the narratives offered so far. Framing the history of sex education through a concern for sex work and sex workers, and acknowledging the normative and epistemological assumptions inherent in their exclusion, points to an unquestionable blind spot, a nothing that is actually something. The value of the lives of the sex workers is depicted as incomparable, on these accounts, to the value of everyone else, which is perhaps exactly why I want to center their value in understanding sex education here. Even while sex workers are acknowledged in these stories, their own experiences are not given the same space or authority in making sense of the purposes of sex education that is extended to others. Certainly, it is not *only* sex workers who are left out, which makes this project incomplete itself, but, to the extent that sex work is positioned as especially contentious within, if not entirely unrelated to, education studies, it is to this form of labor that I commit my own work. Exploring the experiences of the sex worker enables a better understanding of the work sex education does in organizing life in the United States and around the world, and the import of that work itself. Most importantly, though it should *not* have to be said, sex workers are indeed living, breathing, beings whose lives inherently matter. Their exclusion from educational discourses represents education's own exclusionary foundation.

In order to resist this exclusion, I ask: What would it look like to read the era in which sex education emerged from a concern with the life and experiences of the sex worker? To this end, I move forward with this examination of sex education for three reasons. First, again, is my desire to affirm the existence, experience, and knowledge of the sex worker and the legitimacy and value of her work. In doing so, I also hope to identify a different view of sex education's history and, with it, an alternative understanding of its relationship to violence, including its relationship to mitigating violence. Finally, taking the experiences of the sex worker to be invaluable to the history of sex education more explicitly justifies a concern for the contemporary relationship between sex work and sex education and all but requires of us—those interested in intervening upon violence—to imagine something "otherwise." In an effort to stay focused on these aims, I have bookended each chapter with the words of sex workers, of all kinds and of all genders, and of all levels of notoriety, and with very little commentary from myself. While these are not the only spaces wherein the voices of actual sex workers are present, they are the most evident, and I want to be clear about why I have made these choices. I do not want to speak *for* sex workers. I do not want to even attempt to have the kind of knowledge/experience that might allow me to interpret their voices. My intent instead is to both frame the scholarship presented as important *because of them*, as opposed to suggest that they are important because of the scholarship. I also intend to present statements about sex work by sex workers that are disruptive of the stigmatizing discourses that circulate discussions of sex work, particularly within education, and to make it all but impossible for those interested in sex education to dismiss as irrelevant or unimportant: those on agency, pleasure, power, survival, acceptance, and joy.[40]

Without a new way into the critique of sex education, we are likely to remain bound to the same discourses that have failed to lead to real change in how individuals, *all* individuals, and communities, *all* communities, experience and participate in processes of education that facilitate nuanced, broadened, and deepened notions of sexuality. I am serious about the way in which our contemporary attitude toward sex education is dangerous and has real effects on real people's lives inside and outside of the school setting. And I am serious about the connection between such an attitude about sexuality and education and the traumatic and deadly events that continue to plague our world. In pushing for alternative pedagogies and moving beyond sex education policy, I hope to make space for different critically informed practices that privilege the epistemologies of those most harmed by our current educational policy and that need not wait for legislation to be implemented. In this way, I believe that while critique is at the heart of this project, so too is the generative nature of such critique. As Cathy Cohen writes, scholars interested in such questions ought to "take seriously the possibility that in the space created by deviant discourse and practice, especially in Black communities, a new radical politics of deviance could emerge."[41] Indeed, it is my hope that the small constructive component of this project, no matter how imaginative and impossible, might, at the least, inspire anyone or any community that feels the weight of education's assumptions about the role, and kind, of sex in schools as harmful, to resist and reconstruct educational experiences in new ways that dismantle the logics that enable and normalize such harm in the first place.

What follows constitutes a more detailed exploration of sex education's ideological history and policy evolution, and the relationship to violence present in both. Chapter 1 again calls upon Foucault, as well as critical insights from the field of Queer of Color Critique to reorient the history of sex education around the history of sex work and to ruminate on what happens to our understanding of sex education, as a national project, when it is considered in this way. The lessons I take away from doing this work makes up the focus of Chapter 2, wherein I attempt to situate federal interest in sex education within this history of the United States' relationship to colonialism, slavery, and racism, heteropatriarchy, and the emergent privileging of the capitalist, and ultimately neoliberal, subject within American society. Here I extend my use of Queer of Color critiques and engage with additional Queer of Color scholarship, as well as postcolonial and cultural studies. Chapter 3 offers an argument for seeing the project of federally funded sex education as a form of state-sponsored violence by evoking the concepts of state violence and biopolitics. This chapter is "inward" looking, focusing on the way federal sex education policies in the United States maintain and naturalize violence today within its own borders and also addresses the "problem" of the human at stake in these policies. The following chapter, however, shifts the gaze "outward," considering the relationship between the state violence trafficked in sex education against those within the United States as inherent to its foreign affairs and thus implicating it as part of a general, global contradiction between national policies on sex education and the treatment of sex workers. Chapter 4 therefore offers an international view of sex education policy in the United States.

Finally, left with what I argue is little reason to maintain sex education as it currently exists, Chapter 5 offers a justification for moving "beyond" policy-oriented change and, instead, for calling upon the tradition of Black radical imagination to guide the positing of new pedagogical demands that more deeply resist and undermine the systems sex education policies currently uphold. Within this justification is an argument for the essential and inherently productive nature of critique, and, as such, an argument for resisting prescriptive suggestions for policy makers, practitioners, scholars, and communities. Given the patronizing and over-extended reach of imperialist powers perpetuated by such "constructive" work, I instead return to the experience of sex workers and, in the short Conclusion, offer an impossible, impractical, unrealistic demand, and deeply held personal desire, for what I imagine could be a nonviolent, non-Enlightenment-based homage to the intimate relationships between sexuality and education themselves. My hope is not to tell others what to do but to humbly offer something that might spark in others the desire and demand for a world different than this one.

1

Origin Problems

Josephine Baker, the infamous entertainer who left the United States for France, once said about how such a move impacted her, that she was "amused"; "What did I see first? Men and women kissing each other in the streets! In America, you were sent to prison for that. . . . This freedom amused me. . . . In the theaters, women could show themselves without clothing. I could not believe it, so I bought dozens of pictures of nude women."[1] Later, about her sexuality and sexual experiences, she'd add: "I'm not immoral . . . I'm only natural."[2]

In this chapter, I turn away from a rehashing of the "origins" of sex education's federal inception and, instead, seek to articulate a view of sex education in relation to an institution and practice that is largely ignored, if not explicitly scorned, by education: sex work. In order to do this, I rely upon Foucault's concept of problematization as well as critiques of systems of subjectification from those doing Queer of Color scholarship. These discourses frame my look back, so to speak, and provide a previously unconsidered view of why sex education exists as a worthy investment for the US government. I have chosen to focus on federal sex education policies rather than all other kinds of policies and programming not because those do not matter—they do, perhaps even more directly than federal programs—but because it is the relationship between the US state and sex education that is at the heart of the questions about sex work and violence that I laid out as vital in the Introduction. Further, taking this approach allows for new pedagogical questions and concerns about the possibility of using sex education as a space for intervening upon violence that might be of value for those interested in such work.

Because of my interest in examining discourses surrounding institutions engaged with sex education, I want to further clarify my use of Foucauldian problematization. My use of this framework is grounded in the way it centers absences and silences within dominant discourses. More so, it is valuable to me because it asks *not* for certainty but, instead, for *disruptive understandings* of what has previously been deemed a certainty. This again requires an openness to difference that is, I think, sorely lacking in considerations of sex education's value. Foucault's commitment to critique, or what he describes as "constant checking," allows us to remain in an "ongoing" exploration of the biopolitical discourses and conceptualizations with which we operate in the world and, therefore, to resist the complacency that often attends the discovery of a historical "fact."[3] So, this chapter aims not to offer the *right, real, proper history* of sex education but to pry and hold open a space for interrogation and alternative meaning-making that matters in every sense of the word.

This chapter also relies significantly upon Queer of Color critiques. As the name suggests, Queer of Color critique is derived from a critique of Queer Theory. While Queer Theory is itself founded upon a critique of the liberal subject, or of the idea that the "typical" or "standard" subject is inherently rational, autonomous, and heteronormative, it is subject to its own critique related to intersectionality. For many, Queer Theory's critiques of normativity center whiteness and a certain middle- to upper-class politics that continue to marginalize nonnormative lives. In light of this, Cathy Cohen asserts the need for what she calls a "left framework of politics" that "unlike civil rights or liberal frameworks, brings into focus the systematic relationship among forms of domination, where the creation and maintenance of exploited, subservient, marginalized classes is a necessary part of, at the very least, the economic configuration."[4] Queer of Color critiques generally take up this leftist project and work to respond to marginalization and erasures by asserting the necessity of accounting for certain genealogies of thought about normativity, especially those built by women of color. Roderick Ferguson and Chandan Reddy write that "the decisive intervention of queer of color analysis is that racist practice articulates itself generally as gender and sexual regulation, and that gender and sexual differences variegate racial formations. This articulation, moreover, accounts for the social formations that compose liberal capitalism."[5] That is, the critiques offered by Queer Theory that focus on sexuality are situated within Queer of Color critiques as overly reliant upon a critique of heterosexuality,[6] such that they neglect the ways race, gender, sexuality, and class are historically and ideologically co-constitutive of each other, especially when understood as situated within legacies of colonialism and neocolonialism, slavery, and modern capitalism.[7] As Kyla Wazana Tompkins says, Queer of Color critics, despite their many divergences, contrasts, and antagonisms, conjure "queer theory from the heart of these other histories."[8] Queer of Color critiques amount to what I see as a nexus of analytical and experiential critiques of the most dominant and violent processes that make up contemporary human existence: patriarchy, capitalism, neoliberalism, colonialism, globalization, racism, ableism, and, most essentially, the rational human subject.

To the extent that these processes are inherent to the project of public education in the United States, Queer of Color critiques are slowly but surely beginning to appear within educational discourses. And, when they do—when it has been brought in by careful and dedicated scholars, most of them queer people of color themselves—it has immediately palpable implications for education studies. While there has been a longer genealogy of Queer of Color scholarship around pedagogy, broadly defined, it is only within the past two decades or so that even sporadic attention to schools, as institutions in need of analysis, and to queer students of color within such systems of education, has been paid. In his introduction to what is one of the first collections of Queer of Color scholarship on and about queer students of color and Queer of Color critiques of schools, Ed Brockenbrough writes that the most salient intervention the field makes into education studies is through its epistemological questions. He offers two questions, to be specific:

(1) How can queer of color epistemologies interrupt hegemonic processes of knowledge production, and (2) how can these interruptions inform transformative pedagogical work that benefits queers of color specifically and anti-oppressive educational scholarship more broadly?[9]

The call to act that Brockenbrough poses here is one that asks scholars of education studies to explore the scholarship that exists well beyond its typical disciplinary boundaries, as the full fruits of such labor promise novel articulations of liberatory pedagogies. He writes, "like the eclectic analyses of social reproduction in queer of color critique more broadly, educational scholarship must begin to cover wider spans of socially reproductive practices that shape the experiences of queers of color."[10] This project takes up this call. Further, though, I also want to position it as part of a broader effort to bring educational spaces into the view of the vital critiques that Queer of Color scholars have and continue to offer those interested in dismantling the many systems that make violence possible. It is not just that education studies have yet to engage fully with Queer of Color critiques, but that Queer of Color scholarship also has yet to take systems and institutions of education as serious components of the logic they so often aim to undo.[11] The possibilities for education that lie within the work made possible by Queer of Color critiques are endless, so this chapter highlights just one: a new line of questioning for sex education.

Shared Interests

In the Introduction, I offered a glimpse into the reasons for being concerned with the relationship between sex work and sex education, given the historiographical discourses that circulate within education studies. There are many more examples of the centrality of sex work to discussions of sex education at the time to the point that it is very difficult to find an account of the events surrounding its inception as a federal program that is not concerned with the sex worker. For example, there are the words of President Woodrow Wilson to consider. In a "special statement" from a 1917 edition of *Keeping Our Fighters Fit*, a book written with the help of Fosdick to justify the creation of the Commission on Training Camp Activities and to introduce an education about sex to the troops, cited earlier, Wilson writes, "The Federal Government has pledged its word that as far as care and vigilance can accomplish the result, the men committed to its charge will be returned to the homes and communities that so generously gave them with no scars except those won in honorable conflict."[12] We know, though, based on the context, that the idea of "scars" utilized here refers to the sinful climate the prostitute brings about. Situations that allow for such evil must be gotten rid of, it is argued, certainly so that America can prove victorious, but also so that, in the long run, men can return home and serve as proper husbands and fathers within their families and communities. Thus, the federal government envisioned its sex education as a way to help preserve the heteronormative family against the threat of the diseased prostitute, not simply for the sake of eradicating a health problem.

In 1922, the surgeon general of the US Public Health Service released a manual, in collaboration with the US Bureau of Education, edited by Benjamin

C. Gruenberg, the assistant director of educational work for the US Public Health Service, titled *High Schools and Sex Education*. In the foreword to the manual, the commissioner of education, John J. Tigert, and the surgeon general, Hugh S. Cumming, wrote,

> The importance of education along the lines of what is sometimes called "social hygiene" has long been evident to all those interested in the welfare of boys and girls. It was the war, however, that revealed the immediate urgency of this work. Now as before it is essential, both for preventing the destructive venereal disease and for insuring the best use of their creative impulses, that our boys and girls be wisely directed to an understanding and control of their sexual energies.[13]

This call for sex education programming for children in schools comes out of a program to prevent soldiers from being corrupted by prostitutes and the threatening morals their very existence affirms. They continue: "We hope that this publication will be of substantial assistance to those high-school teachers and principals who are earnestly striving to make our boys and girls into more effective, more useful citizens, and that . . . it will contribute to the rearing of a healthier and happier generation."[14] Schools are thus responsible for fulfilling the promise of future national happiness, which depends on a certain view of the family which itself depends on a certain tacit view of the prostitute.

Given education's general lack of concern for the sex worker here, Queer of Color critiques also matter for unpacking the existence of sex education insofar as they are so often *explicitly* grounded in a concern for that labor and for those who participate in its many iterations.

Perhaps most notably, Roderick Ferguson's foundational *Aberrations in Black* begins with a story about a sex worker:

> She is disciplined by those within and outside African American communities, reviled by leftist-radicals, conservatives, heterosexuals, and mainstream queers alike, erased by those who wish to present or make African American culture the embodiment of all that she is not—respectability, domesticity, heterosexuality, normativity, nationality, universality, and progress. But her estrangements are not her own. They are, in fact, the general estrangements of African American culture.[15]

Likewise, in *Funk the Erotic: Transaesthetics and Black Sexual Cultures*, L. H. Stallings offers a reimagining of the idea of sex work itself that challenges the way it has been defined through Western colonialist assumptions about knowledge and being, so brilliantly asks:

> For what is the point in having a pimp/ho degree (PhD) in English if not to create a word hustle that can reimagine cultural and linguistic spaces in which laborers (those who trade sex acts), cultural producers (those who represent and depict sex), sexual intellectuals (those who critique one of the aforementioned or both), and the superfreaks (those who perform all of the work of the previously mentioned sex workers) can resist and riot against heteronormative, capitalist, and puritanical uses of sexuality and cultural together, as opposed to in opposition to each other?[16]

Stallings understands the relationship between sex, sexuality, and work as playing an essential role in organizing contemporary discourses around power that, should power itself be reimagined, must be reconsidered beyond the constraints of Western colonialist and imperialist knowledge systems. This relationship is not accidental to questions about power and knowledge but *imbedded within them*, whether we acknowledge it or not.

A final example of the centrality of sex work to the theorizing of Queer of Color critics, no matter the question at stake, can be seen clearly in José Esteban Muñoz's classic *Cruising Utopia*, wherein sex work is discussed as an alternative space that enables economies that challenge the norms set by capitalism for sexual behavior. He writes that sex work is an

> alternative economy in which flesh, pleasure, and money meet under outlaw circumstances. This economy eschews the standardized routes in which heteronormative late capitalism mandates networking relation of sex for money. This economy represents a selling of sex for money that does not conform to the corporate American sex trade always on display for us via media advertising culture and older constitutions such as heteronormative marriage.[17]

The presence and experience of sex workers here is *not* tangential, and certainly not at all irrelevant to questions of knowledge. Indeed, Muñoz carefully shows that "The hustler-john relationship represents a threat to these other naturalized performances of sex for money, in part because it promotes contact between people of different classes and racial backgrounds."[18]

There are many reasons why those studying education in general and sex education in particular balk at calls for sex work to be considered as part of the conversation, or even at calls for it to be considered as a legitimate form of labor, as these discussions from Queer of Color critics hold. Too often, though, this disregard is justified either on the basis of sex work's relationship to exploitation and trafficking in public discourse or by virtue of the tabooed nature of almost any discussion that holds children and sexual agency in proximity to each other. To be clear, I understand the ways in which sex work does indeed take this form, especially for those deemed "children" by the US government and laws. There is an important conversation to consider around the role of sex work in the lives of queer youth, too, especially those facing housing insecurities. However, as Queer of Color critiques show here, and as will be expanded upon throughout this project, reducing sex work to a form of exploitation does not sufficiently account for the fundamental ways in which sexuality and knowledge production are guided by capitalist discourses, even in schools, and even in sex education. Questions about sex education cannot be separated from a consideration of sex work if the very understandings of sex and sexuality used in the former are precisely the ones that enact the latter's exclusion.

In what follows, then, I rely upon a narrow set of authors writing specifically about the experiences of sex workers in the United States in the late 1800s and early 1900s. As with everything else here, there are many other voices that could and should be added to this, especially ones from outside of the United States, but I have limited myself in this way in order to emphasize the uniqueness of the tensions around race, gender, sexuality, and class present in the States at this time.[19] Through these secondary sources, I explore the history of sex work in this moment of time with the explicit intent of contextualizing sex education's creation and implementation within this history, and not the other way around.

Lessons from Vice

In the context of the United States, one of the most compelling ways for thinking of the presence of sex work at the turn of the twentieth century is by understanding it as undergoing a shift in public meaning and significance. As Ruth Rosen notes, "Prostitution had not always seemed such an urgent problem"; throughout what is now commonly called the "colonial era," the significance of prostitution was far less important for community leaders than other deviant practices, like adultery in any form.[20] Rosen shows that this minimal attention can largely be understood as a result of the deeply masculine nature of colonialism and the ensuing shortage of colonial women in America at the time.[21] However, important to this era was the perceived nature of that vice when it occurred: prostitution was understood as an individual problem, rather than a social or commercial one, and it was believed the women who engaged in "prostitution," which could mean "illicit sexual behavior" in general, were salvageable.[22] Here, with no commercial network or formal exchange of money within it, to participate in prostitution was considered to be participating in one kind of sin among many that could be easily addressed, especially through religion. In thinking about sex education, it is important to recognize that the very thing sex education aimed to eradicate had only developed as such a problem by virtue of other shifts in economic and political cultures far bigger than sexual culture itself.

There is also ample historical evidence that shows how, during the colonial era and well into the childhood of the United States as a nation itself, the concept of prostitution was also central to discourses that legitimized the institution of slavery. Rosen asserts,

> The legal and systematic sexual exploitation of female indentured servants and black female slaves constituted one form of forced prostitution. Female slaves and indentured workers encountered not only forced labor but also the sexual exploitation of their owners. Forced to submit to masters' sexual demands, both groups of women gave birth to children sired by their masters. The law underscored their total lack of rights: a pregnant indentured servant earned a lengthened period of servitude, and the slave saw her offspring become the property of her rapist.[23]

In this way, the use of the word "prostitution" for rape locates prostitution itself as a rhetorical device for minimizing violence against African slaves while preserving the category of "rape" for white women. This is worth highlighting because showing the different usages of the term "prostitute" reveals the highly political nature of the term, as well as its relationship to both sexual and racist oppression and violence. From this view, the very idea of prostitution was used to normalize this kind of sexual and racist violence, which points to its value in producing knowledge systems that, subtly or not, normalize the degradation of

Black women, a practice that we continue to wrestle with, even this long after the "abolition"[24] of slavery. Understanding the history of prostitution in this light suggests that not only is it a politicized concept, but it was conceptually developed alongside the view of the Black woman's body as existing primarily for pleasure, profit, power, or all three, for others.

Prostitution can also be linked to slavery in a second way: apart from being central to slavery's functioning, its eradication directly led to the rise of participation of Black women in increasingly commercialized prostitution. As Cynthia Blair argues, "African American prostitutes were a subset of the black women who struggled to make their way in cities and towns after emancipation and in the early decades of the twentieth century."[25] After the "abolition" of slavery, the United States saw a drastic increase in migration of southern Black men and women to northern urban centers to seek new jobs. However, both Black men and women faced limited job prospects and generally exploitive ones at that. Blair argues that by the turn of the century, many Black women had begun to turn to sex work as more profitable and appealing than the domestic labor positions that were available to them. She notes, "for untold and perhaps unknowable numbers of African American women, sex work provided a viable, often necessary, means of earning money in an industrializing and rapidly expanding urban economy."[26] Further, the rise of commercialized business and industrial centers in the late 1800s generally put women in a precarious position. Being allowed to enter the workforce for the first time in large numbers, however financially appealing, was undermined by sexist attitudes toward women's capacities to work and to generate profit. The effect of these attitudes was compounded by the other effects of industrialization and commercialization on American families in general, as such shifts led to changes in gender expectations and participation in public work.

Women in the working class, of all races, were thus pushed out of the home and, with limited opportunities, often turned to prostitution.[27] Prostitution, in this way, is read by most historians as "a means of survival" for women: "All too often, a woman had to choose from an array of dehumanizing alternatives: to sell her body in a loveless marriage contracted solely for economic protection; to sell her body for starvation wages as an unskilled worker; or to sell her body as a 'sporting woman.' Whatever the choice, some form of prostitution was likely to be involved."[28] This outcome points to a central component of prostitution's history in America, particularly in relation to the regulation of female sexuality: prostitution, and sex work generally, must be understood, at least in part, as a reasonable response to the patriarchal, sexist, and racist nature of urbanization and industrialization in the United States.

As cities and industries grew, the lines between what work was deemed respectable and not, and of course between the private and the public, began to blur in new ways.[29] Specifically, the benefits of industrialization for the working and owning classes precipitated greater visibility of leisure culture. Keire argues,

> As movies, music, and dancing became increasingly common pastimes among young men and women of the respectable working class, the red-light districts, which frequently abutted the cities' theater districts, gained an institutional legitimacy that obscured the difference between respectable and disreputable night-life. Under "liberal" administrations, tenderloin proprietors established dance halls, pool rooms, and restaurants alongside the more traditional brothels and saloons. . . . At the turn of the century, the range of recreation offered in the tenderloins made them as integral a part of the new popular culture as the legitimate entertainment of the white-light districts.[30]

This change had a profound effect on who was able to get jobs and what kinds of jobs were available. Keire notes, "Due to persistent underemployment among poor men, including district men, women had a greater likelihood of securing steady work. Respectable jobs did not, however, prove the only employment for poor families."[31] "District economies," or those economies that developed within and for the sake of sustaining these night-life industries, offered more regular paid work opportunities than "respectable" jobs across race, gender, and class. Keire details how "The wages earned as an unskilled domestic or factory worker, moreover, rarely compared with prostitutes' former incomes. Subsistence wages could not support a young woman unless she lived with her family—and few prostitutes felt they could return to their parents or families."[32] It is of note, too, that while women found steady pay through prostitution, men reaped the benefits of this industry itself by taking advantage of the jobs that it created.[33]

Not only did this new leisure culture depend upon women to generate profit, but it also depended explicitly upon access to women's bodies: whether on the stage, on display, or at a brothel, the use of women's bodies to entertain men both offered income for those left out of more "respectable" jobs and, as a result, made the separation between respectable and non-respectable, or white-light and red-light entertainment, much harder to maintain. This blurring of the moral lines around work contributed to the appeal that prostitution offered women, and this appeal made it difficult for authorities to intervene and thus made it almost impossible for such lines to be reestablished. At the same time, social norms worked doubly to persecute those women for whom respectable jobs were not available or were not as profitable as was satisfying the increasing demand for female bodies.

Blair argues that this phenomenon was particularly salient for Black women, as such women were caught in what she says was a more complicated contradictory position than other women might have faced. Speaking primarily about Chicago, she writes,

> All labored in a society that assumed black women's immorality, scoffed at their aspirations, and mocked their straightforward desire for economic independence. Like other working-class black women, they toiled in a society that held only contempt for the poor, urbanizing African American women who strained in myriad ways to give substance to their freedom.[34]

Within this wage economy, even as more opportunities came into existence for which Black women were theoretically welcome to, prostitution suited the demands of the mainly young and single female Black population better than the opportunities in service work which were more constraining. Thus, "it was precisely the constraints of service work that pushed a wider range of Black women to seek temporary or recurring stints in the sex economy."[35] Given the ways in which their race and gender worked against them within so-called legitimate spaces, prostitution was all the more important for Black women insofar as it brought in money to red-light communities in general, which were largely Black and poor themselves. This economy enabled women to profit, as prostitutes, madams, waitresses, or in other related capacities, from men's recreational activity, and, with such profit, "supported black households that had a difficult time making it any other way."[36] In this way, prostitution existed as a lasting option for many women. Importantly, industrialization also prompted the creation of male populations in search of escape from their laboring days, which has been repeatedly understood by scholars of prostitution in this era as evidence that participation in prostitution did *not* mark a lack of choice or agency.[37] Blair summarizes this finding clearly when she writes that

> Participation in the sex trade resulted from black women's profound economic marginalization. Yet black women were not passive victims of economic displacement. Resorting to prostitution exemplified resourcefulness within Chicago's racially and gender-stratified industrial economy. African American women strategically made use of the opportunities available within late-nineteenth-century sex economy.[38]

Industrialization, and the shifting demographics that accompanied it, thus created much needed opportunities for women, particularly nonwhite women, in the face of their continual exclusions from industrialist projects, and made prostitution an essential component of the work that went into sustaining communities that were otherwise left to fend for themselves.

However, these communities were also *constructed and controlled* from the outside through local and state actions. As local and state governments became increasingly "concerned" with prostitution, segregation-promoting actions were taken, and not just on the basis of race but also one's proximity to prostitution, implicating racialized sexuality in the early institutionalization of segregation, too. The practice of vice districting thus became popular. As Keire describes it, vice districting was "a distinctly American phenomenon, [and] arose out of the United States' creole cultural heritage and the new science of city planning."[39] Notably, the move on the part of local politicians and reformers to begin the work of segregating vice from reputable business areas came as a result of a *rejection* of the public health model for dealing with prostitution: to American reformers, restructuring the city's moral geography mattered more than monitoring the health of "already-errant sinners."[40] This trend is also significant in that it suggests that Prince Morrow initially ended up on the *losing* side of the battle over what to do with prostitution. Skeptical of the possibility that vice districting would actually lessen the presence of vice, Morrow fought against it, but he ultimately lost a 1901 municipal election in New York City as a result, with the idea that a "little hell" was better than a "big hell" winning out among constituents.[41] The segregation of homes and businesses on the basis of vice thus took hold in America by 1890.

Again, vice districting is especially important to the history of sex education because it offers an alternative view into the significance of race to the policing of female sex workers and female sexuality in general. First, it is important to note that the idea of segregation that Americans tend to hold today, as bound to race, resulted from and was grounded in segregation based on sexual reputation.[42] In the late 1800s and early 1900s, that is, systematic segregation happened primarily on the basis of "vice," which, as a concept, was more complicated than referencing a single characteristic or population. Interestingly, Keire shows how the very idea of reputational segregation was seen as in tension with the aims of Jim Crow precisely because it not only allowed for the possibility of racial mixing within its businesses, but, in many ways, it promoted and profited from that mixing. Few places allowed for the mixing of races in the ways that red-light districts did in the early 1900s.[43] Leaders and reformers thus began to envision social reform as requiring the balancing of racial mixing with the presence of vice.[44] However, this tended to lead to the segregation of vice as being seen as synonymous with distance from whiteness, and proximity to non-whiteness, prompting the creation of vice districts in not only poor neighborhoods but those "inhabited by ghettoized and racialized populations," in order to encourage the elite white patrons to at least exercise caution in visiting such spaces.[45] This also meant, as one sociologist notes in 1913, that "the segregation of the Negro quarter is only a segregation from respectable white people. The disreputable white element is forced upon him."[46] Through vice districting, the most stigmatized and seemingly immoral actions were pushed into spaces occupied by those who had already been defined as immoral, all in service of the maintenance of white male respectability.

Given this, it is perhaps no surprise that some of the earliest and largest race riots, including in Atlanta in 1906 and Springfield, Illinois, in 1908, began in red-light districts. These were not purely "race" riots, then—at stake were racialized boundaries of sexuality and class: "Both riots started in red-light districts, were triggered by rumors of a black man assaulting a white woman, and led, not only to the death of black citizens at the hands of rampaging whites, but also to the destruction of black businesses throughout the tenderloin."[47] In fact, it was in direct response to the Springfield riot in particular that the National Association for the Advancement of Colored People (NAACP) was formed, marking this important moment in Civil Rights history as grounded in debates over sexuality and prostitution. In response to these riots, as Black leaders organized to promote varying combinations of integration or uplift within their communities, white leaders were able to justify further racial segregation, including residential segregation policy, by appealing to the seemingly close proximity of racial violence to urban vice.[48] The depth of these tensions can also be seen in the fact that at the other end of Du Bois's "talented tenth" narrative was the "submerged tenth," within which prostitutes existed, pointing to what Blair argues is an example of "the difficulty that many blacks had at the turn of the century in publicly acknowledging the existence among them of women who exchanged their sexual services for financial gain."[49]

As racism took hold of the public discourse around vice districting and segregation, there remained no genuine attempt to eradicate prostitution at the local level, as white men still continually demanded access specifically to Black women's bodies.[50] The general Progressive concern with race and science, then, was in no way separate from Jim Crow sentiments, nor did it seek to include all "Americans" in its efforts at social progress and change. As Rosen carefully shows, this was in part because prostitution was embedded within the web of respectable work: "Economically, prostitution was a source of income to the police, to procurers, madams, doctors, politicians, and liquor interests. Politically, it upheld gender and class divisions."[51] With red-light districts overrepresenting Black women as they remained central to the fulfillment of middle- and upper-class white male desire, Progressive attempts to control vice perpetuated the normative race-based use of Black women's bodies that had been exhibited in slavery and demonstrated a shared interest in racial segregation and exploitation.

Centering prostitution as I have, albeit very incompletely, here, points to a very different way of understanding what was at stake in Progressive-era efforts to combat venereal disease through sex education. Keire depicts this different story beautifully, as she writes,

> Throughout much of the Progressive era, urban leaders in the South, but also in the North and West, addressed racial order and vice control as intertwined problems. City officials and social reformers used the transgression of social norms and the possibility of interracial violence as a rationale for regulating urban vice. The reverse also held true. City leaders used the control of urban vice as a way to strengthen racial and sexual hierarchies.[52]

Rather than understanding prostitution, and thus sex education, through a limited representation of the Progressive era reducible to a time in which social hygiene, science, medicine, and education converged to help address problems of disease and family, as is the case in much of the history around sex education, these authors show the necessity of calling upon other frameworks that complicate this view through a prioritization of racialized female sexuality. For example, Rosen suggests that Progressive-era reformers were uniquely "willing to use the state as a regulator of the nation's morals," requiring us to understand the burgeoning of Progressive policies, including funding for sex education, as bound to the governmental institutionalization of a certain kind of national subject, a point often diluted when focusing upon disease and hygiene. Blair also argues that instead of studying prostitution through the framework of "the rise and fall of Progressive anti-vice zeal," that it needs to be considered specifically through a consideration of the "sexualization and policing of racial boundaries . . . . These processes both predated and outlived Progressive reformers' preoccupation with urban prostitution."[53] Only by such study, and in refusing to adopt those Progressive concepts and narratives in exploring that era itself, can we understand the extent of prostitution's relationship to the history of race in the United States, and thus see sex education's past differently.

Finally, considering vice in relation to sex education points to one other lesson about education itself: with vice districting increasingly being used as a tool for housing segregation, the drawing of districts enabled an ideological collapse of raced spaces and queer spaces, and this impacted schooling just as much as it did everything else. Speaking, as an example, of the South Side of Chicago, Ferguson notes in his own discussion of sex work that "The Chicago School's construction of African American neighborhoods as outside heteropatriarchal normalization underwrote municipal government's regulation of the South Side, making African American neighborhoods the point at which both a will to knowledge and a will to exclude intersected."[54] Vice districting, and the racialized policing of female sexuality, should be an essential consideration for anyone exploring the history of education in the United States in general.

Criminal by Definition

Not to be sidelined, the role of scientific expertise can, through this lens, also be read as justifying the use of vice as a means for adjudicating moral intelligence and subjective validity. Up until the turn of the century, there was relatively little conversation about the role of prostitution in the spread of diseases, but this shifted as languages of science became favored over moral arguments about vice and sin in dealing with prostitution.[55] As doctors and scientific experts gained more voice and power, they worked to publicize the link between prostitution and venereal disease, and, as has been discussed, eugenics provided an authoritative discourse for normalizing this link. The increased criminalization of prostitution enabled scientific experimentation on prostitutes themselves, and thus prostitutes were also some of the first subjects of eugenics in America. This, rhetorician Robin Jensen argues, marks these discourses of science as a strategy for controlling sexuality. That is, behind the allure of calls for science to motivate sex education, a limited understanding of "fact" was produced, namely as "value-neutral."[56] Jensen thus argues that this limitation resulted in the structuring of scientific discourse upon a lack of information.[57] I will argue that this limitation resulted in the structuring of sex education upon something more malignant than a lack of information.

Vice reform, with the Mann Act of 1910 and subsequent local efforts to criminalize prostitution, was successful only at reducing the presence and size of organized prostitution.[58] After all, where would these women go, and what would they do, upon being removed and arrested? The answer was found in an already popular practice: they would go to carceral institutions. In fact, the creation of reformatories for criminalized prostitutes, beginning in 1910, resulted in prostitutes being one of the first groups of people upon whom eugenic experiments and testing for certain alleged genetic defects were carried out.[59] In another important connection to education, these studies on prostitutes were used to construct the idea of "feeble-mindedness," which was increasingly argued as one of the causes of prostitution and thus became a way of further stigmatizing female sexuality.[60] This stigmatization coincided with the emergence of sterilization in state-run institutions. Rosen notes,

> By 1913, twelve states had laws that permitted the sterilization of criminals, idiots, the feeble-minded, imbeciles, syphilitics, moral and sexual perverts, epileptics, and rapists. Such legislation, like reformatories and prisons in which prostitutes were housed, reflected a society that increasingly associated degeneracy with poverty and gradually sought means to control the sexual behavior of the poor.[61]

The cultures of scientific expertise and social hygiene that structure the stories told about sex education's existence, then, are deeply problematic when one considers its impact on those seen as unhealthy, irregular, uneducated, and thus unintelligent. It was not merely a time for more education for some but also a time of institutionalized violence against boundary-crossing others.

Often, this practice of eugenics took the form of sterilization. Jennifer Terry documents in *An American Obsession* that one of the first incidents of sterilization occurred in 1899 in the Indiana Reformatory, a woman's prison in Indiana. The purpose of this practice of sterilization was to mitigate the spread of deviance by making it impossible for anyone with "hereditary defects" to reproduce.[62] Those most impacted by these state-sanctioned actions were: the insane, epileptic, imbecile, idiotic, sexually suspect, inebriates, criminals, paupers, orphan children, tramps, and, of course, prostitutes.[63] The first set of sterilizations was recorded as having been performed on 236 people with these traits.[64] It is of importance that the idea of deviancy, or perversion, used here collapses a lack of "normal" intelligence, having an unpredictable disease, breaking the law, and not having a proper "family," into the same category of life. Further, the label of sexual deviant was attached to that category. To be clear, this reduction of a certain level of intelligence with sexual deviancy, as well as even the failure to be a familied child, represents the ways in which the traits of non-"normal" intelligence, sexual deviancy, and the disruption of the idealized notion of the family come to be so closely linked ideologically that one comes to signal the others, and each signals a literal lack of value and worth to the state. Terry estimates that, conservatively, by 1931 over 12,000 sterilization operations had been performed; to be labeled according to these traits, including to be a prostitute, meant being defined as a criminal and was sufficient for being robbed of the ability to reproduce at all.

By the start of the First World War, then, the fear of prostitution was systemically produced, particularly given the still present concern for "white slavery," which I will discuss in more depth later in the chapter. The preexistence of this fear became fodder for those who needed ways to convince others of the danger of vice districts, as it was now attached to the possibility of military victory. That is, the First World War enabled a shift in rhetoric about and in federal power to regulate prostitution. Terry argues, "Martial rhetoric sounded superb when mobilizing a movement, but it took an actual war to eradicate tolerated vice districts from America's cities."[65] Attempting to close brothels, rather than shut down districts, was the rage, but, as is the case with most things, the elimination of certain spaces for prostitution did not in itself end prostitution. Rather, it prompted the relocation and recalibration of its activities:

> The new forms of prostitution that emerged had one specific goal: to avoid police detection. Since brothels and parlor houses could no longer advertise their wares, rooming houses, flats, hotels, and massage parlors became the predominant sites for prostitution. . . . For the majority of poor women, however, the closing of the houses meant increased streetwalking, which was immediately noticed in most American cities.[66]

In other words, the war was a great gift to anti-vice reformers, as prostitution could now be deemed a threat to national security in a way that was not possible before, and it marked a notable increase in power on the part of the federal government to address prostitution.[67] And here, we learn more about the situation to which Fosdick, and eventually the US war department, was responding that led to the first federal form of sex education discussed previously. In this way, war, and the need to affirm the United States' power in the world, enabled the growth of the anti-vice movement precisely because it justified calls for respectability and health that cohered with the stigmatization of prostitutes. Jensen points out, too, that the rhetoric at the time was such that "Women who were sexually available to soldiers were working against the U.S. war effort by potentially infecting them with venereal diseases and enticing them to break their moral codes."[68]

When Fosdick went south—to Arizona, Texas, and New Mexico—in 1916, his concern was with understanding the "moral readiness of the army."[69] From Keire: "What Fosdick and subsequent investigators saw disgusted them. Border towns already had a reputation for raucous red-light districts, but the tenderloins of southwestern cities such as Douglas, Arizona, El Paso, Texas, and Columbus, New Mexico exceeded even the most dire expectations of debauchery."[70] Concerned with what would happen if troops were to be mobilized, the Commission on Training Camp Activities (CTCA) was created to find ways to distract soldiers from prostitutes and red-light districts. This concern also led to the section on prostitution to be added to the Selective Service Act of 1917, in which the secretary of war was given the ability to "do everything by him deemed necessary to suppress and prevent the keeping or setting up of houses of ill fame, brothels, or bawdy houses within such distance as he deem needful of any military camp."[71] Keire argues that this policy enabled the federal government to establish rules about morality for American citizens and, ultimately, to put the power of the federal government behind the movement to eradicate vice.[72] Jensen also adds that because the CTCA refused to educate white women, and continually characterized African American girls and women as "inherently immoral and overly sexual," it *actively created* a public that was uneducated and thus further reliant upon men for their health and knowledge.[73] That African American men, of whom there were some in the camps at the time, were also excluded from being a focus of this education perpetuated the notion repeatedly emphasized by the US government at the time: African American men, too, could be reduced to their ostensibly uncorrectable sexual urges.[74]

In trying to understand the involvement of the federal government in the project of sex education in relation to prostitution, we can better understand the depth of blame placed on women across races, while in different ways, for the sexual vices of men.[75] This is important because it demands that the concept of female sexuality also be defined as always racialized and also because it shows how white women's fates were bound to those of Black women. This incentivized white women's interest in sex education because it was posited as a way for white women to distinguish themselves from Black women without having to address the inherent racism in sex education. This conclusion is evidenced in the language used at the time, which was notoriously confusing and vague for popular audiences. Jensen argues that much of the discourse around sex and sex education at the time was purposely "clouded by ambiguity" so as to strategically appease Victorian notions of respectability at the time without violating that illusion through articulations of the belief in the subhuman nature of Black women.[76] This was not mere rhetoric, though— the stakes were high. During the First World War, the CTCA was authorized to intern 15,520 women in federally funded reformatories and homes, a number that does not include those held in jails or quarantined in hospitals for the purpose of eradicating vice and prostitution.[77] White women's ability to distinguish themselves from other women might mean the difference between being confined to a prison and being confined to their family.

Wartime rhetoric also increasingly shifted from discussion of prostitutes as dangerous to women in general as being in need of more surveillance, and experts went so far as to label them in their educational programs such things as "malarial mosquitoes," "used toothbrushes," and "German bullets."[78] Keire argues that these acts forced a "single sexual morality" upon the United States, reduced women to their sex organs, and solidified the inferior status of prostitutes and disease-carrying noncitizens.[79] The work of the federal government under Fosdick and the CTCA on prostitutes and prostitution in the form of sex education for soldiers reveals the project of sex education as a fundamentally anti-woman movement, something passed over by those who assume talk of traditional femininity and family roles signals concern for the lives of women. One of the only ways for some women to distinguish themselves from the "bad" women was to buy into the very criminalization that threatened all women who were in the position of having to make difficult choices about their livelihood and made some women, especially white woman, complicit in the construction of prison industry as a fundamentally racist one. That federal funding for sex education emerges during this time is no accident, then, and instead situates it as part of the criminalization of sex work in the United States.

White Slavery and the Gaps in Sex Education's History

Let us briefly return, though, to one founding narrative of sex education's relationship to prostitution, white slavery, which was a fear-based source of political intervention into sex education between 1911 and 1916.[80] What do we learn about sex education when we take seriously the relationship between the regulation of female sexuality and the idea of "white slavery" that was so widely circulated at the time? White slavery, as an idea, reveals something important about the significance of race to the history of sex education that has, to my knowledge, been only glossed over by sex education historians. While the historical relevance of the push to eradicate "white slavery" has been cited by many historians as part of the justification for the federal government's attitude toward the prostitute, there remains much work to do in unpacking its importance to understanding sex education. There are at least three ways that the issue of "white slavery" can be addressed, all of which overlap: with a concern for "White," with a concern for "slavery," and with a concern for the assumptions required to understand the two ideas together.

"White slavery" was, on Keire's account, generally defined in the Progressive era as "the selling of women's bodies (the 'traffic in women') for the purposes of prostitution."[81] Though the term itself has international origins, it became an increasingly popular term in the United States in the mid-1800s. Keire attributes the rise of the term to the prevalence of economic language during the era, which was dominated by concerns over labor, corruption, and trusts.[82] However, the allusion to race was not accidental: this language was able to "provide white workers with a way to condemn industrial inequities, evoke an artisanal ideal of labor republicanism, and yet differentiate themselves from black chattel slaves in the South."[83] This language was also increasingly sexual in connotation, with the figure of the Black sexual predator, typically male, appearing more and more in Progressive-era discussions—and media depictions—of vice and segregation.[84] As Ferguson argues, the Mann Act was even known euphemistically as the "White Slave Traffic Act" and "was designed to protect white men's access to white women against the presumed desires of black men. Black critics, in turn, charged that the law made white women the only worthy beneficiaries of state protection, while black women were the legitimate prey of white men."[85] It must be noted, though, that the discourse of white slavery did also condemn a whole slew of other immigrant populations, too. As Bromfield argues, "The ideologies that were imbedded in the white slavery movement were multidimensional but ultimately worked to maintain white Anglo-Saxon superiority and racial hegemony over newly arriving Italian, Eastern European, Chinese, French, Irish, and Jewish immigrants during the third U.S. immigration wave."[86]

Justification of anti-vice laws usually employed melodramatic narratives about what forced women into prostitution, what kept them in such positions, and what distinguished victims from others, typically along racial lines.[87] Most importantly, though, there is much debate in historical accounts of prostitution and the Progressive era over the extent to which "white slavery" actually existed en masse. Rosen finds some evidence for it in sources that show that between June 1910 and January 1915, 1,057 people were convicted of white slavery in the United States.[88] In a Progressive-era survey that asked 6,309 prostitutes why they had entered prostitution, 7.5 percent listed white slavery or extreme coercion.[89] One of the most significant questions, then, is why "white slavery" was considered such a desperate problem at the time, given these limited numbers. Rosen argues that while the melodrama surrounding the issue itself may have been significant, even if it was not truly such a threat, that rhetoric made it possible for the mere mention of white slavery "to deflect attention away from the very real social and economic factors that led women into prostitution. The class guilt of middle-class Americans for conditions that gave rise to prostitution was projected onto a few villainous white slavers, typically represented as foreigners."[90] The idea of white slavery, she argues, existed and gained popularity for its use as a way for white people to acknowledge prostitution without recognizing their relationships to it. Further, as Jensen also exhibits, "the number of native, white Christian victims of the slave trade was comparatively small. Many women forced into prostitution were Southern black women sold into northern states, Asian women sold into Western States, Jewish women sold into north-eastern states, none of whom were generally the focus of white, Christian middle-to-upper-class societal concern."[91] Thus, "white slavery" was a racialized, gendered, *and* classed construction, calling attention to those whose class did not disrupt the high-class norms associated with whiteness.

It is perhaps for this reason that much of the task of policing white slavery consisted of addressing the importation of women into the United States, often by means of the Mann Act.[92] Racially speaking, it is of importance to acknowledge the fact that many of the women who were imported during the Progressive era were from China and Japan and, according to the research presented by Rosen, endured truly slave-like treatment. When the Chinese Exclusion Act of 1882 was passed and made the importation of Chinese prostitutes more difficult, it also increased their value, making the selling of girls by their families the primary source of forced prostitution for Chinese women.[93] Take, for instance, this retelling of the white slave market that emerged in San Francisco as a result:

> There, Chinese white slaves were directly brought from ships to endure a humiliating physical examination by potential buyers. In an apartment called the "Queen's Room," young girls were subjected to the kind of dehumanizing objectification that Africans had experienced upon landing in the hands of southern auctioneers. Many of these girls, often as young as eleven and twelve, ended up as slaves of the infamous crib system—viewed by one reformer as the worst form of American sexual slavery. He described the cribs as "small rooms opening into inner passages by means of a barred

window and door, which is kept locked by the manager, the key being given to men as they apply to him. Within these little cells, scantily furnished, are kept young girls, most of them Chinese and Japanese, but some of the European and American. They have little light or air, are rarely allowed to leave their rooms, and the manager receives their money."[94]

The conditions under which prostitutes operated at the time were varied, but if anything akin to "slavery" was happening, it was less to white girls and women than to those Chinese women who were transferred across the ocean as sexual commodities.

As Judy Yung argues in *Unbound Feet*, the desire for Chinese women, particularly in western America, was driven by the lack of women in general in the West at the time.[95] At a time when white prostitutes were moving north from Central America and West from other eastern cities for the purposes of sex work, wherein one could make almost five times as much than if one worked as a domestic laborer, Yung notes that "Chinese prostitutes were almost always imported as unfree labor, indentured or enslaved."[96] This most often involved kidnapping or being sold and purchased for profit by one's own family members to someone who would then sell them to the person who would become their new master. It was largely for this reason that the Alien Contract Labor Law of 1885 was enacted to protect indentured servants; however, this law did not apply to Chinese prostitutes. Instead, they were subject to large-scale abuse and even resale when they did not meet the expectations of their owners.[97] Others, though, were immediately sold into parlor houses, "luxurious rooms on the upper floors of Chinatown establishments that were furnished with teakwood and bamboo, Chinese paintings, and cushions of embroidered silk."[98]

Within these parlor houses, there were at least two kinds of labor occurring. First, the sale of sex was only open to certain patrons. Here, Yung explores the way the value of these women was dependent upon racist and xenophobic depictions of them: "the 'exotic' atmosphere, the relatively cheap rates, and the rumor that Chinese women had vaginas that ran 'east-west' instead of 'north-south' attracted many white patrons."[99] However, some women were also sold to entertain through song and dance. No matter what, though, these women tended to be valued primarily as property.[100] This meant they were more scrutinized by their owners for their appearance and behavior and were much more limited in mobility than other turn-of-the-century prostitutes because of their status as indentured servants. Chinese prostitutes were also subject to institutional segregation and racism, much like those from Central America as well as nonwhite prostitutes in general. Yung argues that "both groups of women were ghettoized and, in accordance with the racial prejudice of the day, consistently singled out for moral condemnation and legal suppression, even though white prostitution was also prevalent."[101] That is, there was a hierarchy of prostitutes from the perspective of the law that operated upon the assumption of the criminality of nonwhite prostitutes, an assumption that was not extended to White prostitutes in the same way. However, this hierarchy was often reversed when it came to valuing these women, as the more taboo or illegal, the higher the price to be demanded. The prostitution of Chinese women was exacerbated in the early 1900s to fulfill what Yung calls "a specific need in Chinese bachelor society" alongside a declining population of Chinese prostitutes.[102] Chinese women's worth in the sex trade rose from as much as $6,000–10,000 in gold.[103] Like other areas, Chinatowns, too, were subject to the "nation's purity crusade," amplified by the idea of "white slavery," but to very different ends.[104] When the Mann Act was passed, for example, its blind spot in relation to voluntary prostitution made further, more targeted legislation necessary, prompting California to pass the Red-Light Abatement Act in 1913. Raids of spaces wherein prostitution was suspected ensued. Yung shows, though, that the first raid occurred in a Chinese brothel.[105]

In understanding the history of sex education through prostitution, then, and in taking race seriously as an analytic for that understanding, the significance of the word "slavery" in such discourses also grows. It is troubling, then, that there is almost no attention paid in stories of sex education's history to the relationship between "white slavery" and the institution of slavery itself; instead, it is as if such a connection is either obvious or unimportant. Either way, this neglect only makes sense if the imagined historical issue is viewed in a way that makes slavery irrelevant to that history. On this point, and following in the footsteps of Darlene Clark Hine, Blair argues that "any discussion of black women's sexuality must take into account both the communal memory of sexual abuse and the continuing centrality of acts of sexual violation to the structure of racial inequality well into the twentieth century."[106] If this position is taken seriously, and if these people, who existed as full, complex, important people at the time in which the language of "white slavery" was taking hold in the American imaginary, are granted legitimate space in this story, it is devastating to see them continually dismissed in such stories. The idea of "white slavery," therefore, enabled a facade of concern for women's lives at the time, but instead "materially worsened the lives of prostitutes" and worked hand in hand to support racial segregation.[107] In this way, "white slavery," as a widely circulated frame for limiting what constitutes a life worth protecting through racist sexual norms is essential to understanding the existence of federal sex education. If "white slavery" mattered to those calling for sex education, it was because it allowed for the federal government to assert its benevolence while maintaining racist tropes about Black female sexuality, as well as Chinese female sexuality, and female sexuality in general, in order to do little to actually intervene, because, after all, it fueled an industry that was a site of growing capital wealth.

Sex education's history might well be told, then, as a story about "white slavery." Roberts argues that "America has always viewed unregulated Black reproduction as dangerous. . . . A persistent objective of American social policy has been to monitor and restrain the corrupting tendency of Black motherhood."[108] In tying the history of social policy in America to the dehumanization of Black womanhood, Roberts convincingly demonstrates the consequences of social policy for how dominant understandings of sex, sexuality, and reproduction, including what it means to be sexually educated, have been structured against the lives of Black women. In her reading of the history of Black female reproduction, she argues that this process of dehumanization can be traced back to the founding fathers' ideological and material visions for the United States. She writes, "The white founding fathers justified the exclusion of Blacks from the new republic by imbuing them with a set of attributes that made them unfit for citizenship. The men who crafted the nation's government, such as Thomas Jefferson, claimed that Blacks lacked the capacity for rational thought, independence, and self-control that was essential for self-governance."[109] This belief is pertinent to how we analyze and understand the history of sex education because both makes normal what might otherwise be seen as confoundingly pernicious: its existence as an extension of the government's attempt control sex work. In order for this connection between sex education and sex work to be so systematically avoided as a serious part of sex education's very existence, it requires some kind of allegiance with the idea that sex work is fundamentally immoral, or that it is tangential to the experiences of students in educational spaces. My point is that this nascent allegiance to this belief is, as Roberts shows, a racist one, too.

Finally, the focus on "white slavery," both during the Progressive era and in stories of sex education's founding, often leads to a neglect of the very real presence of indigenous women in these histories, spaces, ideologies, and, well, prisons. This group is perhaps one of the most overlooked populations in studies of sex education in the United States,[110] and, as a result, direct connections between sex education and the colonization of indigenous groups in these borders remain almost entirely unexamined and therefore desperately in need of attention by those serious about addressing the relationship between sex education and violence. The experiences of Native women *must* be included in any analysis of sex education's existence. Native women's experiences reveal some of the most drastic and pervasive cases of sexual and gender-based violence and, as a population, have been stigmatized and delegitimized to the point of erasure, and their absence in these histories is in desperate need of addressing.

Silencing, erasing, and neglecting Native women are part and parcel of the history of the United States itself. Andrea Smith has spent much of her career pointing to the use of silence to minimize, if not entirely erase, any sign of Native women's suffering. Silencing is an extension of violence in this way. The assumptions about worth and belonging in the United States were first established through the erasure and displacement of indigenous peoples, which included the rape of indigenous women, the theft of indigenous children, the killing of indigenous men, and the eradication of indigenous models of kinship, sexuality, and community. Sarah Deer's work on sexual violence in the United States offers one of the most detailed depictions of the centrality of colonialism and the trafficking of Native women's bodies in the history of prostitution on what is now "owned" by the United States. She writes specifically about how "Removing Native women from their lands, homes, and families was an essential factor in depriving them of their personal liberty."[111] Of additional importance are her experiences in the absolutely evil places that were Native American boarding schools at the time, which existed purely for the sake of more erasure and silencing and were fraught with sexual violence against children of all ages and genders.[112] Deer writes how, by the beginning of the twentieth century, if anything akin to what was brought to mind in the use of "white slavery," existed, and it was the treatment of indigenous children, as they were regularly kidnapped, stolen, beaten, and trafficked.[113] Of course, the military training camps built at the time were often built upon stolen, Native land, further implicating them in what Deer calls "a different kind of attack on tribal cultures."[114] Though there is almost no accounting for indigenous people in the stories told about sex education, it must, at the very least, be acknowledged that the erasure of these people from our understanding of sex education's founding is far more suggestive of an allegiance with this history of erasure than with anything meant to disrupt it.

It is also worth noting that Rosen is the only author here who explicitly discusses sex education. This observation comes in her discussion of the Progressive reaction to prostitution: sex education, Rosen argues, was one of many attempts at social reform that emerged precisely as a way to address sex work, backed mainly by social hygienists.[115] This fact points to the limits of these histories themselves and, if we shift perspectives momentarily to educational concerns, raises the question of why education as an institution is absent from these narratives despite its centrality to the era. However, whether cited or not, these histories ask us to reconsider sex education drastically. From within this history, sex education is understood, to use Rosen's words, as part of the network of reforms that "increased state repression of the most visible evidence of commercialized vice, and increased state control over the lives of prostitutes."[116] To understand sex education through both the history of sex work and the experiences of the prostitute is to expose new contingencies of sex education itself. Through this story, we can see the way in which sex education was a racialized, classed, and heteronormative project dependent upon a particular relationship to sex work.

What, then, are the implications of this history for sex education and for the relationship between education and sexuality? In an interview about her less-famous autobiographical book *Gather Together in My Name*, Maya Angelou recalls a different interview, where her own history of sex work was brought up in conversation. Of this moment, she says,

> The woman who interviewed me, who I knew slightly, said "Maya Angelou, how does it feel to know you are the first Black woman to have a national best seller, non-fiction, second book nominated for the Pulitzer and to know that at 18 you were a prostitute?" It was like a kick in the stomach. However,

there is this. You must always be careful who you call out. . . . I said, "Ah, but there are many ways to prostitute oneself. And you know a lot about that don't you dear?" Whereupon they went to break.[117]

On this note, then, what are the different lessons that this history of sex work might have for us? In the next chapter, I explore this impact by considering its relationship to the broader political and economic interests of the United States.

2

Small, but Mighty

A Little Funding for a Huge Cause

In the previous chapter, the story of sex education's existence as a federally funded project was reoriented around a question about its relationship to the history of sex work. Here, I will explore questions that this different understanding of sex education produces, particularly in terms of its existence as a federally funded project. Thus far, I have left untouched the ever-present assumption that sex education was worth investing in. My reason for doing so stemmed from an interest in troubling the very assumption that this form of investment is either normal or good. Calling into question stories about sex education's history, and reorienting them as part of sex work's history, brings us, I hope, to a point wherein such a troubling is not merely interesting but essential in understanding sex education today. It puts us face to face with realities that otherwise sugarcoated might go unappreciated, like that of Sylvia Rivera and Marcia P. Johnson, who "decided it was time to help each other and help our kids. We fed people and clothed people. We kept the building going. We went out and hustled in the streets. We paid the rent."[1] These sex workers changed the world, which suggests something about the significance of maintaining their exclusion.

In this chapter, then, I turn to this assumption about sex education's inherent worth by exploring how its ties to sex work situate sex education as in relation to the federal government and its own long-standing imperialist legacies. The legacies that I explore here are colonialism, slavery, and capitalism. There are others to be explored, for sure, but these legacies are the ones I find most explicitly enacted in the attempt to create sex education as an extension of the federal government's interest in controlling sex work and sex workers. Again, Queer of Color Critiques have much to say about these legacies, and because of the centering of those who might otherwise be deemed irrelevant to stories about our past, like the sex worker, they offer a way of learning different aspects of these legacies that might otherwise be overlooked. More specifically, they help frame sex education as part of a broader attempt at policing sex work through careful attention to the processes of subjectification that is valued, legitimized, normalized, and depended upon. In highlighting the relationship between these legacies and the processes of subjectification they relied upon to justify and maintain their own legitimacy, we can make better sense of the significance of sex education's existence as a federally funded attempt at reigning in "deviant" sexuality.

Colonial Logics and Capitalist Aims

The alternative story of sex education's purpose includes plenty of evidence of its relationship to colonialist logics and settler-colonial interests. Despite the strength the illusion of colonialism as a thing of the past presently has over American imaginaries, Queer of Color scholars, most of whom depend themselves upon the rich literature done within indigenous, cultural, diaspora, and postcolonial studies, consistently take this illusion to task in their work deconstructing other myths about contemporary categories of racial, sexual, gender, class, and ability differences. Front and center in this process is always the acknowledgment that the project of colonialism is enacted through European, heteropatriarchal justifications of superiority, as well as through the construction of what Maria Lugones calls the 'modern/colonial gender system,' which is imposed through the theft of indigenous land and the use of violence to control the lives of those who inhabit(ed) such land.[2] Importantly, these experiences are *not* entirely unique to the colonial encounter that took place on what is now the United States; it includes the land that is now labeled North America generally, Central America, South America, the Caribbean, and the Pacific Islands.[3] Additionally, Queer of Color Critique works to honor the fact that colonialism was constituted by practices of forced migration, slavery, displacement, the shattering of kinship formations, genocide, religious persecution, rape, and sexual violence, among many others.[4] The problems analyzed within and addressed by these critiques are, therefore, predicated on an understanding of their historical, ideological, and material connection to these practices and the lasting legacies of colonization.

Queer of Color Critiques thus offer an analytical framework through which the history offered in the previous chapter can be explored in terms of its own relationship to settler colonialist logics. When I say "colonialist logics," I am referring to forms of knowledge and systems of knowledge production that extend colonial values and norms well beyond the confines of any so-called colonial era. This includes any moment in which rationality is defined in a way that justifies or normalizes the "binary division between the colonizers and the colonized," as Stuart Hall describes it, or, to follow Aníbal Quijano, "the control of a specific form of labor" as, "at the same time, the control of a specific group of people."[5] The term "settler colonialism" refers, then, to an extension of colonialism that perpetuates colonialist logics about "natural" claims to land and bodies that, while seemingly "less" violent and certainly less explicit than public understanding of "what happened in the past," remains dangerous and deadly in its legitimization of the destruction of indigeneity today. Additionally, it functions through the overdetermination and control of what constitutes knowledge and by linking the idea of the human to those whose capacities for attaining and using knowledge are aligned with colonialist aims. Sex education's relationship to sex work can be understood as complicit in these logics in the following moments.

First, of course, is the fact that the federal government began investing in sex education during a global war. As seen earlier, the federal government explicitly situates sex education as essential to wartime efforts, precisely because it would theoretically help preserve the "American" way of life in the face of global threats. In undermining that way of life, sex workers themselves became threats, and thus their eradication becomes patriotic and morally justified. This should be understood as an example of settler-colonial logic: here, racialization and patriarchy work together to uphold the paternalistic belief that not only was the land upon which the domestic military camps were established *not* itself stolen land, but also that the further occupation alongside the driving out (or removal) of "unwanted" bodies was justified on the basis that doing so is essential to any attempt by the "West" at maintaining global control and power.

More specifically, Smith and Lugones's work on the heteronormative nature of colonialism details the ways in which colonialist logics hinge upon racial and sexual norms. If we consider the moment in which sex education emerged as a federally funded project in the early twentieth century, it becomes immediately evident across literature and documentation that central to the United States' general domestic interests was the desire to police populations through the enforcement of a particular conception of racialized sexuality. By "racialized sexuality," I again mean to highlight the interrelated ways in which categories of race and sexuality have been constructed historically and ideologically, particularly in the West. I could just as easily discuss this in terms of "sexualized race," though, as the order of the categories of identity is not meant to signify the importance of one over the other. Instead, I only wish to carry forward the work of the likes of Siobhon Somerville and Roderick Ferguson who have powerfully shown both the ways that racial segregation helped to "ensure the sexual purity of white women and the sexual mobility of white men,"[6] and how "compulsory heterosexuality in the twentieth-century United States has drawn much of its ideological power from the ways it buttresses as well as depends on naturalized of racial difference."[7] The point here, though, is that this construction of racial difference, inherent to the purpose of sex education, is itself a lasting mark of colonialist logics. It maintains assumptions about belonging in the United States that were first established through the erasure and displacement of indigenous peoples, which included the rape of indigenous women, the theft of indigenous children, the killing of indigenous men, and the eradication of indigenous models of kinship, sexuality, and community.

That part of this colonizing was furthered through the use of kidnapping, stealing, and purchasing of African peoples cannot be understated, either. Central to the function of slavery in the United States was taking land from others, taking bodies from other lands, and putting the latter on the former and calling it "natural." Lest those new inhabitants of the stolen land be deemed legitimate owners, they too had to be dehumanized, stripped of their culture, traditions, education, and spirituality, and redefined as mere tools, always disposable and always replaceable, for economic growth. As Adrienne Davis writes, "the economy of American slavery systematically expropriated black women's sexuality and reproductive capacity for white pleasure and profit."[8] Whereas African men were deemed stronger workers (or stronger animals), African women were hypersexualized in order to normalize the need to control their bodies, denounce their knowledge and experiences, and, ultimately, justify raping them to maintain the labor force. This is a distinguishing feature of Black women's histories, as Davis describes most powerfully: "Enslaved black women gave birth to white wealth."[9]

As they became foundational to the establishment of the United States' economic infrastructure and emergent international power, albeit in different ways, both African and indigenous women were subject to the whims of Western, white men, and this is clear in the discussions surrounding sex education's founding when sex work is considered. The very people, non-Western, nonwhite, female, as well as nonnormative kinship systems, whose erasure was inherent to colonialism, became symbolic of the immorality plaguing the Progressive era. By the beginning of the 1900s, then, the criminalization of deviant bodies and ways of being became increasingly institutionalized and were deemed necessary for the well-being of both the white family and the white nation. That this is the moment that the very idea of "sex education" as it exists in the United States was introduced and institutionalized is not an accident, and that this idea perfectly supports the maintenance of this vision of the United States and "American" life must be seen as intentional, too. Take, for example, Blair's description of prostitution in Chicago between the 1880s and 1910s. During this time, Black women are largely offered only unappealing, dangerous, or low-wage laboring positions, making it more profitable to engage in sex work, which was itself more profitable depending on the more deviance the worker was willing to perform or enact, in order to survive. Blair shows how the state punished those caught doing this but also provided the context under which such economic exchanges were increasingly profitable, worthwhile, and accessible to such women. This is an erasure coupled with a source of income that mirrors colonial intentions. With the emergence and expansion of vice districting and racial segregation, the federal government works hard to perpetuate the idea that those who participate in such activities are dangerous to the moral and political stability of the United States, particularly because of the threat prostitution poses to the legitimacy and purity of the traditional, heteronormative family.

The eugenic values inherent to calls for federally funded sex education also suggest its participation in settler colonialism. Eugenics, when applied to populations, normalizes the specifically colonial presumption that the growth of one population depends upon the erasure of another. Sex education is argued to be valuable precisely because it can do the work of helping "educate" the public about the validity and necessity of these erasures. The federal government also took as authoritative the science that upheld these practices as true, and good, and rational. Because part of these seemingly scientific truths was underscored by "evidence" of the great threat posed to those who might think otherwise, "white slavery" itself is therefore also a point of association between sex education and settler colonialism. This view is strengthened by the anxieties around racial mixing that are present in eugenics and "white slavery." As Cedric Robinson suggests, the introduction of the slave trade to the "New World," which he sees as a "most natural step" in securing Spanish and Portuguese economic power, complicated the stakes of racial mixing.[10] Whereas many colonizers saw African slaves as harder workers than Natives,[11] which furthered colonialist desires to remove Native and Indigenous populations, many colonizers also collaborated with "native elites" in order to have them at their beck and call should African slaves ever take up arms themselves.[12] These mixed messages and contradictory understandings of their situatedness thus heightened concerns around racial and ethnic mixing itself, despite the often contradictory ways in which such mixing through reproduction could move one up or down on the colonial hierarchy. If we see eugenics as a reflection of these continued concerns across races and ethnicities, its targeting of sex workers, among other similarly oppressed people, suggests that the legacy of colonialism is itself very much present in the calls for federally funded sex education.

These colonialist logics also normalized the ever-strengthening system of capitalism. The racial and gendered foundation of labor that colonialism depended upon became, in many ways, the very racial and gendered foundation of capitalism. There are, then, at least two ways to explore the place of sex education within this history, given its relationship to sex work: first, through a consideration of the sex workers themselves, and, second, by an exploration of the more general trend toward the normalizing of the limited notion of work ethic and profit making. When critiquing capitalism, however, there is always the danger of reproducing colonialist narratives. Indeed, many Marxist critiques of capitalism, particularly those developed within the West, have done so by centering their discussions of socialism and Marxism around those lives who were already affirmed by colonialism in the West. As Cedric Robinson argues, such critiques "incorporated theoretical and ideological weaknesses that stemmed from the same social forces that provided the bases of capitalist formation."[13] There are other, non-Western, non-European lineages of capitalist critique, however, that have contributed to modern conceptions of socialism that are often neglected in such discussions. Further, the West has never seen its own true experimentation with socialism either, which means that there are other lessons about socialism to be learned from those who have put these ideas into action themselves in different ways. While this project does not explore those, in addressing the relationship to capitalism that is at stake in sex education's approach to sex work, I do understand part of that relationship as being another instance of colonial imposition. More specifically, it is the alignment with the nuclear family, Protestant work ethic, and, ultimately, the privileging of a specific kind of reproductive labor that binds sex education's colonialist logics to its capitalist ones.

The nuclear family is essential to the project of sex education, and certainly was, too, at sex education's development. It is also an important tool in both colonial and capitalist projects for measuring civility and productivity. The nuclear family's primary function was, as many have detailed, to maintain a societal structure in which Western European colonists could ensure their own superiority by virtue of their reproductive relations themselves. At the core of this idea was the desire to undermine indigenous, slave, and non-heteronormative kinship formations and, in doing so, justify the criminalization and erasure of those who drifted from these norms. Capitalism emerged as a reflection of this hierarchy, positing not only the Western family as superior to others by virtue of the head of household, the male's, preordained ability to work hard and thus deserve the fruits of his abilities, especially when those abilities meant controlling other bodies so as to increase productivity and profit. Likewise, as Ferguson writes, this meant that capitalist relations also came to structure the private sphere itself, so that the white family was the natural benefactor of the labor of others, and the labor of others was justified because of their distance from this white ideal.[14] The development of capitalism in the United States is therefore *not* a purely economic event, but one that was made possible by the always already present exploitation and devastation of Black and indigenous lives through the alignment of work with the heteronormative family, such that the ability to perform kinship "properly," or through previously established Victorian-era values, became a marker of one's economic legitimacy. Sex education's persistent obsession, from the get-go, with this family model suggests its complicity in the development of capitalism in the United States along the very lines arguably drawn first by colonialist powers.

Part of the naturalization and normalization of this model of the family and the association of all other ways of cultivating systems of care and belonging with deviancy was further enacted by the assertion of a particular kind of work ethic that can be seen clearly within the history of sex education when considering the uneven treatment of various kinds of work, and the value of that work, at the time. This idea of "work ethic" is, according to Kathi Weeks, historically grounded in Protestantism and thus naturalizes "the command to approach one's work as if it were a calling,"[15] the value of work, the view of work as an end in itself,[16] and the view of work as a path toward salvation.[17] This means that essential to capitalist development was the coalescence of meaning around a view of work that took it to be a reflection of one's soul. This works both ways in that work ethic reflects the goodness of the soul *and* the goodness of the soul can thus be interpreted on the basis of one's work and commitment to that work. Weeks adds that this work ethic is therefore always an "ethic of consumption, one that avows the necessary, legitimate, and indeed ethical link between hard work and whatever might count in different economic phases as deserved and responsible spending."[18] Something like prostitution, then, largely because of the disruption it causes, or threatens to cause, the "normal" and "good" nuclear family, is marked as an illegitimate site of labor, and those who make their livelihoods through that labor are also marked as illegitimate. The emergence and lasting power of capitalism, then, was co-constituted by a reduction of human morality to a judgment of one's relationship to capital and work, a reduction that, because of its relationship to both colonialism and the nuclear family, was a racialized and sexualized one.

However, the history of sex work suggests another relationship between sex education and capitalism that complicates the idea that this relationship is merely one-sided, with sex education working as a way of normalizing private lives for the sake of capitalist interests. Instead, as Ferguson argues, capitalism is not merely a *homogenizing* institution; it also instigates the creation of heterogeneity:

> Capital is a formation constituted by discourses of race, gender, and sexuality, discourses that implicate nonheteronormative formations like the prostitute. In addition, capitalist political economies have been scenes for the universalization and, hence, the normalization of sexuality.

But those economies have also been the arenas for the disruption of normativity.[19]

As the historians of sex work discussed previously, prostitution ought not to be understood as merely an irrevocably irrational and evil practice; instead, they show how it was perfectly justifiable given the historical context facing nonwhite women at the time. Situating this within capitalism more specifically suggests that we can read prostitution, especially as something "deviant," as having been *produced by* capitalist formations. Rather than understanding capitalism as merely homogenizing subjectivity around one particular way of life, it also creates an excess, a body that cannot be brought into that process, a heterogeneous subject developed out of capitalism's marginalizing capacity: "Capital, therefore, calls for subjects who must transgress the material and ideological boundaries of community, family and nation. . . . Indeed, the production of labor, ultimately, throws the normative boundaries of race, gender, class, and sexuality into confusion."[20] As the state's actions become more and more aligned with economic interests, instead of creating universal obedience to the sexual, raced, gendered, and class norms that uphold that model, those who "fail" find relief in other ways of being and other models of kinship. This excess therefore becomes the target of moral panic.

In other words, because men must be able to work and because men must be able to *fight* for the federal government, they must be protected from what destabilizes their birthright-like claim to this work and to being able to do it successfully. However contradictory, it is the necessity of work, and the morality attached to one's access to work, that provides the context out of which prostitution is transformed into a "social problem" in the late 1800s/early 1900s. The creation of federally funded sex education can be read, then, as part of a broader socioeconomic-political effort by the state to negotiate racial, sexual, and class tensions in ways that affirm white male dominance and rule. Insofar as sex education emerges as a tool for orienting racialized sexual behavior around a version of morality asserted by Western white male heterosexuals, it participates in legitimizing capitalist class hierarchies. This is also precisely how anti-immigrant sentiments and practices become part of the work of sex education: to the extent that prostitutes are considered to be less-than citizens and many prostitutes were and are themselves immigrants, whether forced or not, sex education also perpetuates the practicality and rightfulness assumed in this ethnocentrism.

Of course, sex education, when situated within a concern for the history of sex work, was described above as primarily serving the purpose of policing *female* sexuality, begging the question of what to make of this story about work ethic and the family that is so often centered upon white male supremacy. Despite the male-centeredness of these logics, it is important to remember and notice that it was ultimately female sexuality that was deemed both the perpetrator, or the threat, to men, *and* the innocent victim in these discourses. The reason that it can be both at the same time is because of the value of one specific kind of labor, of which only women were seen as capable: *reproductive*. Prostitution was a moral threat, and a physical one, too, but it also threatens the claims patriarchy makes to the economy and to the family as the site of the reproduction of the race. Women *did* this kind of work and *did* make decent money doing so, but it was a *nonreproductive* labor, which undermined these claims to power. Sex work was a particularly slippery thing to control, then, because its profits were substantial enough to keep women (and men) involved in the industry, but it contradicted the gender and sexual norms that were supposed to function to uphold men as the heads of household, economically and otherwise. The only way to approach this problem was to continue to maintain a division between women which, though perhaps more fundamentally a division based on labor and thus a raced and gendered one too, was publicized as a division based on morality. Sex education was proposed and enacted for the very explicit purpose of towing this line, which was itself hitched to the desire to control and eradicate deviant sexual ways of being.

Fast Forward: Contemporary Control and Extended Erasures

While the times between the 1920s and the 1980s saw tremendous changes to the structure of modernity and included experimentation with various forms of sexuality education across places, spaces, and bodies, I want to now fast forward to a consideration of the more recent federal funding for sex education, beginning with the Reagan administration. This is a huge leap, and I do not want to minimize what is left out about the extension of the logics discussed earlier into their contemporary institutionalized forms. Because my original question about sex education's purpose and existence was derived from a concern for modern-day violence, however, I am making the choice to put this foundational history as thus far interpreted into direct conversation with the federal policies that have most recently been used to invest in sex education at the national level. There are important lessons to be learned about sex education in doing so.

To this end, it is the Reagan administration that we can thank for causing a foundational shift in how the federal government approached sex education. Infamous for its many socially devastating policies, the Reagan administration utilized sex education policy as one space among many for legitimizing the impacts of such policies. Originating in subtitle G of Title IX of the Omnibus Budget Reconciliation Act of 1981, under the Maternal and Child Health Block Grant, the Adolescent Pregnancy Program is listed as part of a broader attempt by Reagan and his allies to, allegedly, improve the health and material situation of mothers and children.[21] Eventually named the Adolescent Family Life Act (AFLA), the act took a clear position on female sexual behavior and its relationship to the federal state. Of the most concern was the financial burden associated with nonnormative female reproductive practices. That is, while depicted as a concern for children born out of wedlock, the *cost* of them, to both the family and the state, was the most immediate worry. A still common refrain, and a racist and sexist one at that, the story was that teen pregnancy's relationship to increased financial dependency upon parental figures into adulthood was a threat to national stability. Further, the cause for this issue was described as a lack of individual, personal responsibility. Once again, deviant female sexuality is situated as an economic problem, the solution to which—the regulation of that sexuality—could be justified through the same Progressive-era logics around the nuclear family, public health, and worth ethic.

This stigmatization is exemplified in the rhetoric regarding how sex education ought to participate in the improvement of these health and financial problems. Teen mothers, and their out-of-wedlock babies, are depicted as burdens on their families, and while the government does express concern for the physical and mental health effects of being a teen mother, the final word on the stakes is financial. For example, in its reasoning, the act (US Senate 1981, 579) states that

(5) pregnancy and childbirth among unmarried adolescents, particularly young adolescents, often results in severe adverse health, social, and economic consequences, including: a higher percentage of pregnancy and

childbirth complications; a higher incidence of low birth weight babies; a higher frequency of developmental disabilities; higher infant mortality and morbidity; a decreased likelihood of completing schooling; a greater likelihood than an adolescent marriage will end in divorce; and higher risks of unemployment and welfare dependency.

Here, the weight of economic well-being is put primarily upon women and the tension between their productive and reproductive capacities, echoing the same problem for which sex education was originally proposed to address. A notable difference, however, is that the male body is now entirely absent from the story. It is hard to believe that absence would be possible if the original intent of the idea of sex education was not itself to control female sexuality, even if that control was intended to benefit men.

Also, a child's life is here overdetermined by the behavior of the child's mother, again putting the responsibility for the whole family upon women. Further, the conflation of female sexuality and economic well-being is used to justify the call for increased attention to the preservation of the ideal American family, "since the family is the basic social unit in which the values and attitudes of adolescents concerning sexuality and pregnancy are formed."[22] Now, though, financial stability is not just the reason for controlling, judging, and punishing female sexuality but also a euphemism for justifying doing so. This act, therefore, also marks the beginnings of a neoliberal shift in sex education, or the expansion of capitalist logics more explicitly into the realm of social, political, and cultural life and liberal valuations. Finally, this language makes explicit claims about what constitutes knowledge and thus about who should be educated and for what purposes. Just as with eugenics, social hygiene, and public health narratives, the assumption here is that some people just don't know better, and some people *won't ever* know better, leaving education accessible only to those who have the intelligence to be swayed by such education. Increasingly, then, the very idea of education and intelligence is tied to sexual behavior and federal complicity, and the child, who is innocent and lacking agency, must be protected from the consequences of their mother's lack of education. Paternalistic, patriarchal rhetoric pits the future generation's well-being against female knowledge just as it did so before and during the First World War.

Nonetheless, by 1984, AFLA was extended and amended because of the desire "for education and vocational training activities to be integrated fully with health and other services provided by the Adolescent Family Life Act."[23] Here, sex education is not only tied to but justified by the concern for job growth. The evidence used to advocate for this amendment includes this statement about teenage pregnancy and jobs:

> Several studies have shown that teenage parenthood significantly affects the educational attainment of teenage parents and that this, in turn, leads to low-skilled and less well-paying jobs. This tendency is exacerbated by two other common outcomes of teenage parenting: the likelihood of larger family size and the probability of single parenthood. These factors "work together to create significant barriers to economic self-sufficiency for teen parent offspring, contributing to a cycle of poverty which is passed from one generation to the next." The cost to society in terms of public expenditures for health, social services, and public assistance, and the loss of what would have been future economic contributions of teen parents has been repeatedly noted in the research literature.[24]

The purpose of sex education, and education in general, remains as it was: a mechanism for advancing profit and economic growth. Even health, social services, and public assistance are grouped under a concern for public expenditures. These blatant reductions of life to economic terms represent another instance of education and knowledge production being aligned with one's participation in the economy, itself depicted as directly influenced by one's sexual behavior and marital status.

The conclusion regarding the purpose of the act, however, extends its primarily economic concerns and represents once more the ways in which the need to police sexual activity was justified through an appeal to neoliberal understandings of the student as worker, and the parents and family as meaningful primarily as an economic unit:

> The benefits of educational and vocational attainment to young parents and to society are enormous. These services will help to meet the long-term needs of teen parents by helping them to break the cycle of poverty and repeat pregnancy that too often accompanies adolescent parenthood. It is now known . . . that a lack of education and marketable skills are the foremost causes of long-term welfare dependency. The Committee intends to strengthen the on-going efforts of demonstration projects to help adolescents, including adolescent fathers, improve their educational and job status.[25]

As a policy that marks the arrival of a new interpretation of sex education, this source of formalized federal funding is an important moment in the history of sex education as it continues to rest upon the assumption that the federal government's investment in legislating the sexual activity of the public could be done, at least in part, through education in public schools. That is, the public has a vested interest in allowing the government to teach students about sexuality by connecting it to the economy precisely because sex education is, by definition, a mechanism for trying to prevent the disruption of the economic stability of students, as future workers, and their real and imagined families, that uncontrolled sexual activity may cause.

Once again, though, the context that is Reagan's presidency and its relationship to the Christian Right matters to understanding the nature of the relationship between education, sexuality, and the economy here. As Jennifer Terry writes, "By 1980, when Ronald Reagan took presidential office, the New Christian Right had successfully delivered millions of votes to the Republican Party through campaigns aimed at morally cleansing the nation."[26] When it came to sexuality, the primary way that this influence played out in the Reagan era was through the stigmatization of promiscuity, assumed to be prevalent among nonwhite women. Building upon the legacy of the 1965 Moynihan Report, or "The Negro Family: The Case for National Action," which repeated the idea of the Black woman and mother as an incapable, overly sexual, threat to their own children and thus to the future itself—or, as overall unintelligent and ill-informed—Reagan's depiction of the Black welfare queen harkens back to the same kind of moralizing about Black lives that was central to many Progressive-era movements, including those advocating for sex education.

Roberts's work again poignantly details how Reagan's "War on Drugs" was part of a long tradition of demonizing Black women as bad mothers and financial problems.[27] Roberts shows that these rhetorical campaigns were so effective that by 1990, 78 percent of white Americans believed that Black people preferred to live on welfare.[28] Further, Alexandra Lord notes that Reagan's allegiance to the Religious Right, as well as his economic policies, resulted in a great increase in the role of the federal government in sex education during his administration, despite his cutting of other welfare programs. She adds that there is a coherence of ideology present, though, as these policies, or his changes to them, "ensured that federal institutions began to reflect the views of those who opposed both sex education and the sexual revolution of the

1960s."[29] His interest in disinvesting social services, his lack of attention to particular populations of American citizens, including Black working women and also people living with and increasingly dying from AIDS/HIV, and his historical role in enabling the rise of neoliberalism further justify the reading of this act as an extension of the same moral panic over the impact of deviant, racialized, female sexuality on the family and thus the economy seen in sex education's inception.

Not to be outdone, though, it was in 1996, under the Clinton administration, that the same grant that was originally used to fund AFLA, though now located in Title V of the Social Security Act, was restructured to explicitly invest in abstinence education, or sex education that views abstinence until marriage that only reasonable and justifiable sexual behavior. Therefore, as part of the amendment to include a "Separate Program for Abstinence Education" in the SSA, a detailed eight-point definition of abstinence education was offered for the first time and remains intact today.

"Abstinence education," accordingly,

(A) has as its exclusive purpose, teaching the social, psychological, and health gains to be realized by abstaining from sexual activity;

(B) teaches abstinence from sexual activity outside marriage as the expected standard for all school-age children;

(C) teaches that abstinence from sexual activity is the only certain way to avoid out-of-wedlock pregnancy, sexually transmitted diseases, and other associated health problems;

(D) teaches that a mutually faithful monogamous relationship in the context of marriage is the expected standard of human sexual activity;

(E) teaches that sexual activity outside of the context of marriage is likely to have harmful psychological and physical effects;

(F) teaches that bearing children out of wedlock is likely to have harmful consequences for the child, the child's parents, and society;

(G) teaches young people how to reject sexual advances and how alcohol and drug use increases vulnerability to sexual advances; and

(H) teaches the importance of attaining self-sufficiency before engaging in sexual activity.[30]

This definition allows only for the teaching of the importance of abstaining from sex until marriage, the moral, political, and financial consequences of doing otherwise, and places ultimate responsibility upon the individual to maintain this lifestyle.

Much has been made of this policy, and rightly so, as it is amazingly concerning in so many ways, but my interest in it here is because of the way in which the idea of abstinence itself seems to maintain the logics of sexual deviancy as a concern for economic production that we see in the early 1900s. Here, one's sexual practices are only legitimate to the extent that they don't disrupt the norms that structure capitalism's righteousness. Abstinence here is described as necessary for preventing economic dependencies that are seen as undermining these aims. The language of dependency is somewhat different from the language of the nuclear family used previously, though. Rather than being a sign of a *different* logic, this can be read, I think, as a nuanced articulation of the *same* logic if we understand it as evidence of the replacement of the family as the guiding institution of personal and political relationships with the state that has also been documented as shaping the twentieth century. This language also exists to collapse one's value to economic worth along neoliberal logics that mirror the activity that Weeks, in her analysis of the danger of reducing the human to a capitalist laboring subject, is so concerned with. Here, sex, race, and sexuality become foundational to one's ability to labor and, as a result, one's ability to assert their value to the state.

In 2002, under the George W. Bush administration, when the original Title V funding was set to expire, funding was extended for another five years. The extension went on to reaffirm its commitment to the eight-point definition given in 1996.[31] In December 2010, the Consolidated Appropriations Act eliminated funding for all abstinence-only programs, including this one.[32] In the meantime, however, the Community Based Abstinence Education (CBAE) program was enacted in 2000 under the Clinton administration, as part of Congress's Special Projects of Regional and National Significance. Clinton's own relationship to the image of Black womanhood is of importance here. As Roberts again reminds us, Clinton was perhaps just as complicit with perpetuating a view of the Black woman as a leech on the public and as a sexually promiscuous, unintelligent person who exists as a danger to her children. For example, Roberts highlights the fact that demonizing Black mothers who receive money from the state to support their children was central in Clinton's welfare reform proposals.[33] CBAE reasserted the value and necessity of Title V's definition of abstinence education and required all programs funded through it to also adhere to such a definition.[34] As with the language of dependency, this language is both a departure from and an extension of the formative assumptions about knowledge that shaped sex education's creation. Whereas previously deviant, nonwhite women and prostitutes were excluded from the education their existence mandated, which was especially possible given their exclusion from most forms of education more generally, this form of sex education seems to acknowledge that, with the expansion of public education, such an exclusion is far less kosher for the American public. As such, these policies reflect the fact that

> Modern-day racist ideology, then, seems to have shed the assumption that Black people are entirely incapable of rational decision making. Rather, Blacks are more likely to be blamed for the poor choices they make. . . . Black mothers are portrayed less as inept or reckless reproducers in need of moral supervision, and more as calculating parasites deserving of harsh discipline.[35]

From this perspective, these more modern policies do not deviate from previous iterations of sex education so much as they move from maintaining exclusion in general to maintaining exclusion by associating behavior with individual choice. If "deviants" must be allowed an education, and if that education is going to maintain its reputation as a serious institution, the only way to account for deviancy is by offering an education that makes it appear as a choice, and a very bad, morally despicable one at that.

Obama's presidential era included continued funding for programs adhering to Title V's definition of abstinence education through the Competitive Abstinence Education program, which included funding numerous teen pregnancy prevention funds, sometimes more comprehensive than school-based funding allowed for. However, with the passing of the Patient Protection and Affordable Care Act, federal funding for sex education took on a new form. Within this act, and still part of Title V, is the Personal Responsibility Education Program (PREP). PREP allotted each state that applied for funding through it at least $250,000 a year, from 2010 through 2014.[36] The goal of the act remains ideologically the same as those laid out in Title V: reducing pregnancy rates for teenage girls, especially by focusing on those who are "the most high-risk or vulnerable for pregnancies or otherwise have special circumstances, including youth in foster care, homeless youth, youth with HIV/AIDS, pregnant youth who are under 21 years of age, mothers who are under 21 years of age, and youth residing in areas with high birth rates for youth."[37] However, PREP requires that adolescents be educated in different ways than did its predecessors. First, it is comprehensive and allows for the teaching of both abstinence and contraception and requires that the teaching of both be based on other evidence-based programs and "rigorous scientific research," be medically accurate, include discussions of sexual behavior in terms of both abstinence and the use of contraception, discuss sexually transmitted infections, be age appropriate, and be attentive to the cultural context of its students.[38] The emphasis here also, for the first time, acknowledges students as potentially sexually active at the time they are in school, better enabling their sex education to reflect their experiences as such.

Additionally, PREP takes an additional step away from previous abstinence education programs and requires that each program funded must address at least three "adulthood preparation subjects," chosen from this list:

(i) Healthy relationships, such as positive self-esteem and relationship dynamics, friendship, dating, romantic involvement, marriage, and family interactions.
(ii) Adolescent development, such as the development of healthy attitudes and values about adolescent growth and development, body image, racial and ethnic diversity, and other related subjects.
(iii) Financial literacy.
(iv) Parent-child communication.
(v) Educational and career success, such as developing skills for employment preparation, job seeking, independent living, financial self-sufficiency, and work-place productivity.
(vi) Healthy life skills, such as goal-setting, decision making, negotiation, communication, and interpersonal skills, and stress management.[39]

This list offers what many would consider important interventions upon abstinence-only education, particularly in its broadening of discourse on relationships to include those beyond the person with whom one has sex or marries, allows for conversation about issues related to sex and sexuality beyond pregnancy and disease, encourages relationships with parents, and considers a person's future financial success and life goals as related to the project of being educated about sex and sexuality.

Despite this, though, PREP seems to reinvest in a neoliberal attitude toward sexuality and education perhaps more than its "controversial" predecessors. For instance, we see a blatant return to the economic language used during the Reagan era that associates one's financial stability to one's family life, to one's sexual activity, as well as a continuation of the importance of marriage from the abstinence programs to that relationship. Further, the view of the individual that PREP asserts is especially concerning, because, in broadening its understanding of how sexuality and sexual activity relate to the rest of one's life, it reinforces a definition of individuality grounded in self-sufficiency, rationality, and one's capacity to labor and make money, all pillars of neoliberal subjectivity. This is mirrored in both the stated aims of PREP and the subjects to be taught: both emphasize the individual's ability to collect and act upon "medically accurate" and appropriate information, which then is to allow for clear, reasoned decision making that many have, I think rightly, argued to be problematic. For instance, Nancy Kendall has argued that this turn depicts the student as a consumer of sex and sexuality and implies that individual, rational decision making is the standard for adjudicating whether or not one is to engage in sexual activity.[40]

PREP also asserts a definition of sexuality in economic terms. While the act nods its head at community and group differences regarding sex and sexuality, it ultimately doubles down on an understanding of the individual, as an "accurately" informed decision maker and a financially literate worker, suggesting its investment in neoliberalism. In fact, if programs must discuss only three of these points, it is easy for sex education to turn into a lesson on financial stability and career readiness, which is likely to happen in a cultural climate where sex education and its teachers are increasingly under attack for merely talking about sex in schools, which Janice Irvine has convincingly documented.[41] Finally, equally important is the fact that the very next section of the Affordable Care Act following the establishment of PREP restores the abstinence education as laid out in Title V, through 2014.[42] From the perspective of the federal government, then, in PREP's attempt at expanding sex education to reflect a variety of cultural and sexual differences, it invests literally and ideologically in the form of sex education that it seems to replace and furthers the historical commitment to the student and worker and consumer, and a view of sexuality mediated by an economic framework, by reinforcing the relationship between sexuality, family life, the economy, and the job market, through an emphasis on individual sufficiency, intelligence, and control, all qualities of the ideal neoliberal subject, a subject who serves neoliberalism itself. Intelligence is to be displayed in one's sexual activity, and the more one adheres to these standards of sexual life, the more legitimacy and value one has. Of course, then, the more that deviance exists in one's life in relationship to this set of expectations, the larger the threat one is to the state, and thus the more one is allowed to be subject to violence of a racial, heteronormative, or capitalist nature.

As we move into Trump-era policies, what has been true thus far mostly remains the same. In 2016, CAE was replaced with Sexual Risk Avoidance Education (SRAE) grants and was intended to be more discretionary in terms of promoting abstinence-only until marriage education than were the CAE ones. SIECUS again describes this move by abstinence-only advocates as a "rebranding" of abstinence-only programs: CAE proponents "co-opted risk reduction language used by proponents of sex education and the public health community in order to make their programs seem more in line with experts in this field. But the substance of these SRAE programs remains the same."[43] Though some of the language around the definition of abstinence has since changed, and the Title V definition is no longer standard in CAE programs, the current iteration of this funding asserts that the purpose of this funding is "to enable the State or other entity to implement education exclusively on sexual risk avoidance (meaning voluntarily refraining from sexual activity)."[44] Funded through FY2020, these grants do require that medically accurate and age-appropriate information be taught and that discussion of contraception may be included, so long as it "ensures that students understand that contraception offers physical risk reduction, but not risk elimination," and that "the education does not include demonstrations, simulations, or distributions of contraceptive devices."[45] In addition, the topics to be covered in these programs reaffirm the long-held federal assertion that sex education's importance lies in its jurisdiction over public health and economic stability and the neoliberal concept of the individual that was instituted decades ago:

(1) Topics: Education on sexual risk avoidance pursuant to an allotment under this section shall address each of the following topics:

 (A) The holistic individual and societal benefits associated with personal responsibility, self-regulation, goal-setting, healthy decision making, and a focus on the future.

(B) The advantage of refraining from nonmarital sexual activity in order to improve the future prospects and physical and emotional health of youth.
(C) The increased likelihood of avoiding poverty when youth attain self-sufficiency and emotional maturity before engaging in sexual activity.
(D) The foundational components of healthy relationships and their impact on the formation of healthy marriages and safe and stable families.
(E) How other youth risk behaviors, such as drug and alcohol usage, increase the risk for teen sex.
(F) How to resist and avoid, and receive help regarding, sexual coercion and dating violence, recognizing that even with consent teen sex remains a youth risk behavior.[46]

Point A centers responsibility on the rational individual and their ability to prioritize their future in decision making about sex; B doubles down on this by entrenching SRAE in a narrative about the relationship between one's future and one's health; C explicitly claims that nonnormative sexual activity can lead to poverty; D locates the ideal life in "healthy marriages" and "safe and stable" families. As the story goes, E reminds us that sex is about risk and more akin to drug usage than anything else. Finally, F posits a seemingly new and desirable idea—the need to educate students about violence and consent—while nonetheless claiming that it is neither violence nor a lack of consent that is the real threat; it is sex itself. From Reagan to Trump, then, the federal government can be seen as continuing to advance a vision of what it means to be sexually educated that itself maintains the same assumptions about whose lives matter and for what purposes that sex education's earlier advocates set into motion.

Telling Silences

Of course, absent from these newer policies is explicit reference to sex work. Given the historical story I have offered here, it is notable that the sex work has gone missing from these policies. However, this erasure is one that I read as reflective of a more complete naturalization of the erasure of sex work from any thought about what it means to be educated in the United States. She still haunts these policies in their utilization of the very ideas and values that she came to stand in for within discussions of sex education in the early 1900s. She need not be mentioned—sex work need not be acknowledged itself—because her very existence, and the existence of this industry as a whole, is rendered impossible given the parameters set by sex education. Why talk about what does not exist? Why mention what *our* children could never be?

This silence is telling, particularly if we consider what such an erasure itself suggests about the imagined community for whom sex education, and thus education itself, serves. That the sex worker and the institution of sex work disappear in contemporary discourses around sex education, especially given her centrality to the very project at its start, points to a new question, to which the next chapter will be directed: if the understanding of sex education that I offered by virtue of its relationship to sex work remained, as I have argued, intact through the twentieth century and into the twenty-first, what does the perfected erasure of sex work from these discourses mean for the politics of sex education today? What do we miss out on—what do we *miseducate about*—when our sex education cannot even address sex work, or what Eve, a streetwalker from Canada, says is "an answer to a lot of things over the years"?[47]

3

Violent Straightening and the Function of the State

The absence of any consideration of sex work and sex workers in contemporary sex education policies amounts to an erasure that is particularly concerning if we consider, as I mentioned in the previous chapter, what it suggests about who exists in the imagined communities sex education is to serve. More specifically, this erasure seems to me to be particularly troubling precisely because sex work itself has seen a proliferation of new types, modes, forms, and participants, as well as more complicated defenses of its legitimacy, and even some legal wins that point to subtle shifts in the winds around the meaning of sex work's, and sex workers', value in the world today. Indeed, sex workers themselves are very much *part of* the communities we imagine, even if our imaginings do refuse to include them. In *A Taste for Brown Sugar*, the author Mireille Miller-Young shares a story one sex worker shared with her that makes this quite clear. In this interview, Carmen Hayes says,

> I was a nurse. I went to nursing school. I did in-home care, urgent care, front office, and back office work, [and worked] in the field. I started dancing to help pay for school. Because my aunties [and family] couldn't help me along the way. . . . I was also trying to be independent on my own. But I also had an itching for it, because I was always the good girl doing everything I was supposed to. I was always on honor roll and student council. I graduated with honors in school; I graduated with a yellow tassel and a yellow robe, the whole nine.[1]

Sex workers are *good* students, too.

Of course, this is not to say that sex work is by any means normalized now, and it is also not at all to say that there are not serious issues, including safety issues, facing sex workers of various kinds today. What I am interested in, then, is what we can learn about sex education by returning to what I have described as an "original" impetus for federal sex education—the need to control prostitution—and exploring the significance of the complete erasure of the sex worker within contemporary policies. This also implicates more contemporary policy *critiques*, and, to this point, this chapter interrogates the relationship between sex education and sex work today, including scholarly critiques of sex education.

To do this, I will first explore how the logics exposed in the previous chapter rest upon a normative and thus exclusionary concept of the human, which suggests that the processes of subjectification at play in sex education are themselves inherently exclusionary. I will then compare the sexual subjectification that takes place in contemporary sex education policies to what Sara Ahmed calls "straightening" and argue that because of the subjective straightening sex education requires in order for a student to be deemed "educated," sex education can be seen as a form of violence. Additionally, I will offer a reading of this straightening as a form of *state* violence and, from this view, point to what I see as inadequacies in even the more seemingly liberatory or progressive or comprehensive critiques of sex education circulated today.

Rationalizing the Human

Despite all the blatant dehumanization espoused in the aforementioned policies, such policies depend upon a view of the human that is specifically defined so as to justify this dehumanization. To unpack and analyze this concept of the human, I will pay attention to three epistemological assumptions, or assumptions about knowledge creation, that are necessary to believing that sex education as a federal project is one that we ought to value. These assumptions regard what it means to be "rational" and what that definition means for how the body is judged as a result. Ferguson describes epistemology as the study of "an economy of information privileged and information excluded, and the subject formations that arise out of this economy."[2] Rather than taking the exclusion of sex work from sex education as a negligible or innocuous, irrelevant point, exploring the epistemological assumptions at play in this exclusion offers a way of understanding what processes of subjectification are at play themselves. This is both a rejection of the narrowing of epistemology that is enacted through "sociological and national depictions" of knowledge and by the depersonalization of epistemology that occurs in the reliance upon such sources of inquiry.[3] This approach allows us to resist decontextualizing what is happening in these moments by recognizing the raced, gendered, sexual, and classed lines that the claims to knowledge made in these policies draw. I take as primary the idea that knowledge is always a political, ethical, and social construct that exists as a way of distributing power, recognition, and worth, and that it is best understood via a consideration of those excluded from these resources on the basis of their so-called lack of knowledge, intelligence, or education. In doing this work, we arrive at a different take on the erasures under examination here.

In the abovementioned policies, the logics I have described as contiguous with sex education's initial relationship to colonialism, slavery, and capitalism, and the racism, sexism, ethnocentrism, and heteropatriarchy they traffic, also depend upon epistemological assumptions themselves. First, then, we can inquire into these assumptions by interrogating the claims being made about what is rational. Time and time again, these policies link rationality and intelligence with a particular set of behaviors related not just to sexuality but to participation in the economy, too. It is not new to point out how rationality has historically been a source for all kinds of marginalization and oppression, and this has been shown to be particularly true for colonizing practices. One way to think of this is in terms of overdetermination: in general, the justifications for colonial violence and the normalization of its continued existence through settler logics were constructed by overdetermining, or narrowing, what constitutes knowledge so that anyone who doesn't fall into that category can be seen as legitimately in need, or as deserving, of colonial control. Andrea Smith's depiction of this is both classic and powerful. She writes that the logic of white supremacy, as the foundation of colonialism, requires that "colonizers must first naturalize hierarchy through instituting patriarchy. In turn, patriarchy rests on a gender binary system in which only two genders exist, one dominating the other . . . the colonial world order depends on heteronormativity."[4] This is an imposition of an epistemological system built on binaries and hierarchies that are themselves claims about gender, sexuality, race, and ethnicity, and ultimately about who ought to be granted access to full "humanity." Lungones adds that studies of colonialism that reject the heterosexualist and patriarchal nature of colonialism encourage an "epistemological blinding" that hides this role of gender and sexuality in colonial power.[5] This points to cyclical relationship between the establishment of these norms around what it means to be rational and therefore human and the lack of consideration of those norms in the very use of the definition of rationality. A different iteration of this phenomenon is seen in slavery, too, and not only because of the relationship between colonialism and slavery but because of the extent to which the idea of rationality was taken to be so connected to such a narrow view of intelligence that those without it could be used to further the wealth of those who are deemed human, precisely because the idea of rationality was defined *for* them.

In the case of sex education, one of the most prevalent examples of this use of an overdetermined concept of rationality to limit who is considered "human" can be seen in the powerful Cartesian, Western division between mind and body, and the attribution of intelligence to the mind, and the mind only. The concept of rationality inscribed in sex education's history is very much aligned with a particular kind of rationality that intentionally and explicitly locates irrationality, and all of the sin and evil that comes with it, in the body. As Smith shows, these assumptions about belonging in the United States were first established through the erasure and displacement of indigenous peoples, which included the rape of indigenous women, the theft of indigenous children, the killing of indigenous men, and the eradication of indigenous models of kinship, sexuality, and community. That part of this colonizing was furthered through the use of stolen African peoples cannot be understated, either. Central to the function of slavery in the United States was taking land from others, taking bodies from other lands, and putting the latter on the former and calling it "natural." Lest those new occupants of the stolen land be deemed legitimate owners, they too had to be dehumanized, stripped of their culture, traditions, education, and spirituality, and violently redefined as mere tools, always disposable and always replaceable, for economic growth. Again, whereas African men were deemed stronger workers (or stronger animals, without human status), African women were often deemed as having little knowledge so that they could be hypersexualized and therefore physically controlled and dominated, and, ultimately, raped. This was essential to maintaining the labor force. Here, patriarchy, sexism, racism, and colonialism again converge and set the stage for a political and economic system that would be legitimate so long as the very idea of rationality, and therefore the human, remained legitimate itself.

There is plenty of evidence from the history of sex education as a mechanism for managing sex workers to support the idea that this mechanism depended upon, and indeed continues to rely on, a view of the human that is intentionally exclusionary. It is women's bodies that are toxic; it is their bodies that are merely vessels for disease, and sex workers are described as irrational consistently in the process of continuing to see them as such. Fosdick himself regularly used the language of rationality, depicting the soldiers as rational and thus those who threaten their viability as soldiers and men as irrational.[6] Morrow, too, expressed sexual health as a kind of "enlightenment,"[7] and the educational material at the time, including "Healthy Happy Womanhood" and "Keeping Our Fighters Fit," similarly attached the ideal of education to the formation of "normal and wholesome attitudes and ideas in relation to sex."[8] The policies discussed earlier therefore only extend the logics that set sex education into action in the first place.

Together, the concept of the human assumed in sex education policies can be read as defined in such a way that some will never be extended admission into that community. This is arguably the most important connection between sex education's founding and the policies that remain in place today and contributes to the idea that not only is the exclusion of the sex worker in these policies significant, but it can more accurately be seen as marking a more active complicity with her dehumanization. Of course, the trick is that her exclusion does not matter—does not *have to* matter—to the effort to improve sex education, but it was there precisely to ensure she did not matter.

Straightening Violence

There is plenty of justification for interpreting these assumptions as marking sex education as a way of enacting violence upon those left out of Western concepts of the "human." More specifically, the use of the idea of the human in sex education is akin to what Ahmed calls a device for "straightening." Through an exploration of the project of phenomenology, Ahmed argues that our experiences of the world can be understood through a consideration of the way orientations toward objects structure both bodies and spaces in ways that create normative lines for humans to follow. That is, the social norms that are most readily rewarded, as well as those ways of being that are most seriously penalized, socially, economically, and politically, can be understood as the result of continual work, by people and institutions. The nature of this work is what she terms "straightening," or the directing of behavior along certain pathways by idealizing particular objects and offering certain rewards and privileges for orienting oneself toward them. In order to understand the processes of normativity, then, we must understand both how and why certain objects are privileged within certain spaces, and how this privileging then structures what orientations, or ways of proceeding through and existing in the world, are determined as being in line, and others are determined as needing to be fixed. She says that this understanding requires considering what objects exist within close enough proximity to people to be considered as directing one's orientation, paying particular attention to those objects that promise the conferral of a particular identity marker when the orientation toward it is well established.[9] To this, she adds, "We can ask what kind of objects bodies 'tend toward' in their tendencies as well as how such tendencies shape what bodies tend toward."[10] Objects thus provide direction for orientation and, in doing so, establish normative pathways for those seeking particular forms of recognition, inclusion, or acceptance through the attainment of certain identities that follow.

This process shapes bodies by requiring the repetition of certain actions over others, wherein any failure to repeat the actions required for staying on course is deemed a failure. This is the moment of normativity: "What is at stake in moments of failure is not so much access to properties but attributions of properties, which become a matter of how we approach the object."[11] That is, value judgments, particularly of character and worth, are made, by other people and by institutions, not on the basis of one's ability to actually attain the object, but on the basis of one's ability to stay in line with its purpose, and to direct one's actions and thinking toward it. Again, this is understood as "straightening." She says,

> Spaces and bodies become straight as an effect of repetition. That is, the repetition of actions, which tends toward some objects, shapes the "surface" of spaces. . . . Our body takes the shape of this repetition; *we get stuck in*

> *certain alignments as an effect of this work.* . . . *Spaces as well as bodies are the effects of such straightening devices.*[12]

Straightening devices are thus those socially, politically, and culturally reinforced ways of being that produce normative social forms against which the value of one's life is determined.

For example, compulsory heterosexuality

> diminishes the very capacity of bodies to reach what is off the straight line. It shapes which bodies "can" legitimately approach as would-be lovers and which ones cannot. . . . Hence, the failure to orient oneself "toward" the ideal sexual object affects how we live in the world; such a failure is read as a refusal to reproduce and therefore as a threat to the social ordering of life itself.[13]

Compulsory heterosexuality offers people particular objects, including certain bodies and ways of life, as the North Star of action and thought. If I stay on course, pointed in the right direction, I give value to the path itself, thereby signaling my own value. Likewise, racism, as a well-trodden path, is loaded with promises and rewards for those who perform and enable white supremacy through hostile gazes,[14] requirements of submission,[15] objectification, and domestication.[16] This thus establishes a "political economy which is distributed unevenly between others, and an affective economy, which leaves its impressions, affecting the bodies that are subject to its address."[17] Simply put, straightening devices are ideas and institutions that help keep one on track, in line, moving forward, through normative rewards and punishments. As ideological, emotional, and material constraints, these devices can enact a certain kind of violence on those who resist their straightening. The word "violence" is used by Ahmed here in terms of the felt and experienced consequences of dehumanization and delegitimization that attend the requirements that such straightening devices demand. To carry the example of compulsory heterosexuality further, Ahmed contends that queer orientations reveal "the everyday work of dealing with the perceptions of others, the 'straightening devices' and the violence that might follow when such perceptions congeal into social forms."[18] Compulsory heterosexuality, as a straightening device, sets limits on knowledge and behavior in order to cause anything from discomfort to physical violence, or even extermination, for those who resist or refuse to take up the path set by orienting themselves toward heteronormativity.

The organization of human subjectivity around particular norms regarding intelligence and reason in sex education suggests that it is, itself, a straightening device. This rationality takes knowledge to be that which can be understood objectively, universally, and primarily through the human capacity to reason, especially given its demand that it also be understood as distinct and separate from emotion and the body. To be good is to act in accordance with reason and therefore to deserving of recognition as human, and thus of moral value. To be bad is to deviate from these norms, to be irrational, to be consumed by the body, and thus to relinquish any claim one might have to humanity and, with it, any moral value. If you want to be treated like a human, then you must make a choice to be good, it tells us, which means living a monogamous, white-heteronormative, married, child-oriented sexual life and calling it love. Exhibit something otherwise, and you've landed yourself outside of the protections assigned to humans. That is, participate in nonmonogamous, nonwhite, non-heteronormative, nonreproductive pleasure outside of marriage, and reap what you sew. However, Ahmed argues that since straightening devices are put in place to direct, or orient, people around certain objects through promises of well-being, success, and safety, they are ultimately violent insofar as they punish deviation from this orientation. Sex education's existence as a straightening device is therefore precisely what marks its own relationship to violence. Granted, sex work has been, for so long, assumed by sex education, and most of any public education in general, to be so bad, so deviant, that it is almost entirely naturalized as such. This is why sex education doesn't need to address sex work: we've already learned what to think, what to feel about sex work. The very concept of "sex education," then, holds the federal government's interest in normalizing sex work as evil—even when it profits from it—in place. Even if this function is purely "ideological," even if the funding streams run thin or dry, these policies show, perhaps more than anything else, the insidiousness of its hatred for sex workers.

Finally, as a straightening device, sex education can be said as operating through a system of rewards and punishments. Adherence to the ideal object promises happiness: attainment of this form of sexual life is rewarded through money and social status. To marry, to own a home, to have children all offer tax breaks; to be monogamous, to be reproductive, to be domesticated is to be deemed a functioning adult human. We see the language of straightening in any drift away from this norm. For instance, to be in a long-term relationship without marrying is understood as living an "alternative" lifestyle; to be polyamorous is to be "lacking direction" or to be "unwilling to/afraid to commit"; to be "single" is to be "on one's own." These are all deviances, and they make someone "deviant." To not have children is often seen as revealing an incapacity to move forward properly. To not be able to have a child or to not want a child, to have an abortion or to adopt, is almost always translated as a loss, a misstep on the path to happiness; it is not the case that one cannot be happy without a child, particularly for women, but instead that one will never be able to experience the supposedly penultimate experience of happiness and love: the miracle of birth. Always orienting behavior, these statements signal the existence of a proper path for social status; each an act of straightening, these words teach students how to stay on the well-trodden path toward happiness. Sex education teaches that to deviate from the ideal is to take a risk, though it is a risk with virtually no possible reward. In this way, sex education is violent because it forecloses possibilities, demands coherence to a particular set of norms, and stigmatizes and silences all those who resist such coherence.

Human Limits and State Violence

The view of violence offered here is somewhat distinct from more traditional understandings of violence that are particularly easy to circulate within education circles. That is, violence is often thought of, particularly within education, as physical injury. Physical violence, or the threat of physical violence, is the most prominent concern and responsibility of the space, and thus discussions of violence in schools are often reduced to a concern with the physical. I think this framing is particularly prevalent regarding sexuality and race in education. Here, it is bullying, suicide, fighting, and gun violence that overwhelmingly occupy such conversations. This pattern is exemplified in sex education discourses, wherein conversations on bullying and suicide are highlighted as uniquely urgent problems facing those experiencing violence, particularly when it is grounded in anger toward, fear of, or hatred of nonheteronormative or nonheterosexual students. Without intending to diminish the seriousness of these physical violences, I seek to argue for the need to address violences that go beyond physical and visible acts of violence. Instead, I argue for the necessity of addressing epistemological violences, or those violences that justify the more overt and physical ones and thus can easily perpetuate the existence of such violence in its many varieties.

Of course, there are those in education who do pay attention to nonphysical kinds of violence. Paulo Freire is perhaps one of the best examples of someone concerned with both physical and nonphysical forms of violence. In some ways, he helps show how this dichotomy is itself problematic. In *Pedagogy of the Oppressed*, he famously asserts that violence occurs in "Any situation in which 'A' objectively exploits 'B' or hinders his and her pursuit of self-affirmation as a responsible person. . . . Such a situation itself constitutes violence, even when sweetened by false generosity, because it interferes with the individual's ontological and historical vocation to be more fully human."[19] This is why all forms of oppressions are inherently violent regardless of their physicality, though certainly inclusive of it, as is any attempt to disrupt one's project of becoming more fully human. This can, on Freire's account, take the form of prescription, or the imposition of one's own views or ideals upon another in a way that affects their consciousness,[20] the treatment of another or oneself as a mere object,[21] or the general submission of oneself or others, or in many cases both, to the reality of the oppressors.[22]

However, the distinction I make here is one between addressing dehumanization with humanization as opposed to directly addressing violence. For Freire, as well as the works of the likes of bell hooks, Henry Giroux, and Maxine Greene, the solution to violence is almost always a deep affirmation of the value of the human. I will instead put Ahmed's work in conversation with Sylvia Wynter's critique of the idea of the human in order to make a case for the potential value of wandering off the "human" path in working to bring about breaks within and away from dominant systems of knowledge. As such, it is not the case, I argue, that the labeling of dehumanization as violent means that it is humanization that is the solution. It is necessary to consider the ways in which dehumanization is not encapsulating of all forms of violence a being can undergo. Rather, I will argue that the reduction of the experience of violence to solely the feelings associated with having one's humanity questioned misses the ways in which humanity itself may be understood as the problem.

Sylvia Wynter's critique of rationality is essential to understanding how the concept of the human motivates violence around the world. For her, the disruption of the various and intertwined systems of oppression that structure the lives of the marginalized, including the systems of colonialism, slavery, and capitalism discussed earlier, depends upon a disruption in the order of knowledge upon which such oppression rests. And this is a task that requires a radical reconsideration of the way such an order defines what it means to be human. More specifically, Wynter argues that part of the way in which marginalization happens is through the grounding of particular determinations of what it means to be human in claims about human nature, which, she argues, has come resulted from a shift from religious justifications to secular ones. With this shift also came a turn toward race-based distinctions and away from gender-based ones. In this ideological history, the ordering of meaning in the Western world erased an entire group of people for whom neither distinction offered systematic power: women of color, particularly non-Western women, who were instead relegated to the status of native savage other.[23] This means that the epistemological assumptions upon which sex education depends, a hundred years ago and today, are where violence thrives. It is in the assumptions about rationality and humanity that made those who were most likely to engage in sex work at the turn of the twentieth century inherently unfit for literal existence, and therefore *at least* justified the construction of sweeping policies to mitigate the threat they posed to the nation itself, including sex education policies. If the nation is at stake, though, it is the federal government that bears at least some responsibility for this violence.

To take this one step further, I would like to argue that, given its relationship to the federal government, this legacy of sex education points to its existence as a form of *state violence*. The concept of state violence has its own history; however, I will remain committed to theoretical framework upon which I have been dependent thus far. In his work on the history of governmentality, or the history of the processes and practices that allowed for a reorganization of power that resulted in various forms of population control and disciplining, Foucault describes the "state" as something that itself has been "governmentalized."[24] Whereas the family had previously done the work of governmentalizing, the emergence of "population" as something to be measured, surveilled, and controlled, turned this work over to the state.[25] The management of the population is the practice of government that coalesces into an idea of the state, though he importantly notes that the state is not really a tangible thing. On this he writes, "But the state, no more probably today than at any other time in its history, does not have this unity, this individuality, this rigorous functionality, nor, to speak frankly, this importance; maybe, after all, the state is no more than a composite reality and a mythicized abstraction, whose importance is a lot more limited than many of us think."[26] The state can and does have real effects on our lives, and its effects are also unevenly distributed and experienced. Nonetheless, it is "an order of things" that is itself governed by that which upholds it.

Additionally, Foucault writes that the individual is essential to the state, as of course is the population, and maintains its own power by requiring adherence to a particular norm in order to benefit from what the state has to offer. He, therefore, writes that the individual is in a unique relationship to the state because individuals are only important to the state to the extent that they engage with its power. That is, individuals can impact the state, then, but the significance of that impact is always interpreted by the state as making that individual valuable or disposable: "It is only insofar as an individual is able to introduce this change that the state has to do with him. And sometimes what he has to do for the state is to live, to work, to produce, to consume; and sometimes what he has to do is to die."[27] This rationality of the state is what Foucault labels biopolitics—it is a political rationality that administers human life.[28] It is not accurate to say that all biopolitical practices are violent, but we can consider biopolitics to be the essential logic through which the state justifies violence. This is the meaning of "state violence" that I am invoking in interpreting sex education's own relationship to violence. As a straightening device, sex education enacts a biopolitical rationality that directly supports the governing of the population that upholds the power of the state itself. Because this rationality depends upon a purposefully drawn line about who, quite literally, gets to live (and how well they can live) and who should die based on what it means to be a good, rational, human, sex education helps govern the population by institutionalizing state interests. To call upon humanization to remedy this violence is therefore more likely to redraw the line in a different way, if it has any impact on this rationality at all. This does not mean such work is not important, but it does suggest that it is not sufficient.

On Resisting the Need to Throw the Baby Out with the Bathwater

To conclude this chapter, I want to explore some of the more powerful contemporary critiques of sex education that have shaped modern-day understandings of the limits of sex education by mobilizing this view of sex education's relationship to violence. The purpose of doing so at this moment in my discussion of sex education is because it is precisely the relationship to state violence that I have centered here that makes sex education so concerning as a federal project and therefore is the measure of understanding the efficacy of other critiques and proposals attempting to address violence themselves. There are other ways of interpreting and measuring these critiques, to be sure, and situating them within a discussion about state violence may be unfair given that state violence is not typically a concern within these discourses. Instead, these scholars largely set out upon their studies of sex education with the aims of understanding its limits within a liberal democratic society and of proposing ways of readjusting sex education in order to make it either more amenable to contemporary identity issues or less stigmatizing itself. As such, these scholars have shaped my thinking in ways that are not captured here. Before offering my own critique of these critiques, then, I want to simply say that my own commitment to understanding sex education and to trying to figure out what the hell to do about all the sexual, and always racialized, violence in this country was formed through serious engagement with this scholarship and is only possible because of the doors these scholars opened for me. The concerns I have with this scholarship are the result of the permission to feel fed up and frustrated that I found validation in while engaging with them.

Within education studies, the prevailing discourse around sex education has traditionally been one rooted in liberal democratic theory. That is, attention to sex education as a legitimate topic for educational theorists specifically emerges late in the twentieth century as an attempt to understand how education about sex, gender, and sexuality could (or could not) be justifiably kept as an essential part of compulsory public education within a "democratic" society. For example, David Archard and Amy Gutmann's research on the relationship between democracy and education situates sex education as a theoretical problem for democratic education. Archard, who importantly set out to justify sex education's very existence, argues that sex education is necessary for a democratic society because, in teaching about sex and sexuality, citizen's own autonomy would be "maximized," and this maximization is essential to a key principle of a liberal democratic theory: liberty itself.[29] Gutmann also locates the "controversial" nature of sex education as resting in a tension between "individual freedom and civic virtue": How do we, in a democratic society, balance the desires and values of the individual with the collective "good"?[30]

As it relates to democratic education, then, she argues that the most "wise and legitimate" approaches to sex education will require sex education in public schools, with the provision that parents can exempt their children on the basis of principled opposition.[31]

In response to these approaches to studying sex education, many educational theorists since have challenged, and continue to challenge, this discourse by challenging the inherent legitimacy, or the normative value, of liberal democratic theory, and its traditional principles of autonomy and liberty, itself. Josh Corngold, Paula McAvoy, and Lauren Bialystok, each working within this area, present their own distinct and nuanced arguments about the relationship between sexuality and education in public schools in ways that represent this kind of challenge. Corngold specifically resists the deference afforded to parents within traditional liberal discourses, especially that of Gutmann, offering a justification for sex education through a concern for the rights of children and their developmental needs.[32] Further, in a critique of liberal conceptions of autonomy, particularly those resting upon an understanding of autonomy as individual sovereignty, he argues that sex education presents an important opportunity for helping students understand their autonomy as "embedded," or as connected to their ability to be a democratic citizen.[33] While perhaps less a condemnation of liberal theory than an attempt to redefine its key principles, Corngold offers valuable critiques of this tradition that have helped call that tradition into question more broadly.

Similarly, McAvoy raises questions about the *content* of sex education and concerns about the lack of engagement with such questions within the liberal tradition. Like Corngold, McAvoy is skeptical of the efficacy of defining autonomy through individual choice-making and of the narrowing of sexual activity to what she says is merely a consideration of "whether or not to have sex, with whom to have sex, and what kind of sex we have with them."[34] She attempts to expand human sexual behavior to include all other experiences that relate to one's life as a sexual being, including how one dresses, the variety of other intimate relationships one engages in, and those sexual behaviors that do not put students at risk for pregnancy and disease at all.[35] Instead of teaching strictly about sex acts, she argues for what she calls "structured paternalism," or state determination of some aspects of sex education, given the extent to which children, especially girls, experience sexual exploitation.[36] Speaking with a more concrete concern for the role of parents in sex education practices in a liberal democracy than McAvoy does, Bialystok explores the ways in which parentally determined exemption allowances, which allow parents to remove their children from any mandated sex education provided in schools, align with the values of such a society. Bialystok is herself situated in the Ontario, Canada, context, and her exploration of sex education controversies in Canada offers an important addition to the way the so-called global West attempts to mitigate the tensions that emerge around rooting democratic aims in rights-based discourses, particularly when attempting to extend rights to both parents and children. Her argument is that, at some point, "when there is good cause to believe that respecting parental rights will violate the rights of at least some children, a blanket solution is in order." This blanket solution equates to something akin to what McAvoy defends, albeit for different reasons and with different purposes: a defense of the state's own right to make sex education, when guided by liberal principles, compulsory.[37]

More skeptical of the promise of liberal democratic principles and practices, there have been, especially in the past two decades, many significant interventions into such discourses. Essential to moving sex education scholarship within, and often beyond, education studies into new, promising spaces, these scholars have opened new doors for considering the many aspects of sexual identity that make liberal frameworks for justifying and detailing sex education unsatisfactory if not damaging. Cris Mayo's critiques of liberalism's commitment to freedom and equality have arguably led the way in these conversations. Mayo shows how such a commitment has continually failed sexual minorities in at least three ways: by limiting discussion and understanding of sexuality to "a matter of private freedom," by failing to account for the way such structures benefit some more than others, and by remaining uncritically attached to the institution of marriage.[38] At stake in each failure is the recognition of non-heteronormative ways of being and a disruption of the constant deference to both "male power" and "traditional gender roles."[39] A passionate advocate for challenging such structures—and this includes those enforced in schools through law—Mayo has targeted not only the institution of marriage but gender binarism and heterosexism, too. This work is bolstered by detailed research showing the influence of the Christian Right on sex education, not merely through its idealization of heterosexual marriage and the traditional gender norms it depends upon. Instead, as Janice Irving shows, the Christian Right's ability to redefine talks *about* sex as sexual *acts* themselves, establishing a mood of fear and paranoia that inhibits the willingness of teachers to teach sex education adequately.

In order to articulate a vision of sex education that resists these pressures and opens up spaces for a more liberatory kind of sex education, a turn to desire and ambiguity has dominated scholarship in education studies on the subject. Most compelling has been Mayo's call for centering conversations of "pleasure, perversity, and community" in sexuality education, a practice that might undermine normative notions of female sexuality, call attention to the role of sexuality in capitalist markets, and move us toward a more nuanced and complicated conception of education itself.[40] Arguing that "desire is the bridge between what is and what might be, disrupting stale patterns and creating new formations," Mayo adds that desire is also necessary to *education* because it is what ultimately "binds communities, and stimulates learning."[41] When human sexuality is more fundamentally related to desire, or Eros, it can thus be seen as making possible both a different kind of education and political action. This argument echoes Deborah Britzman's own call for understanding that sexuality is "central to the capacity for human curiosity, for living a vital intellectual and social life, and for our capacity to attach passionately to knowledge, other people, and life projects."[42] Sexuality, Britzman argues, ought to be understood as "the first condition for human curiosity and hence the first condition or force for human learning. Simply put, without sexuality, the human would not desire to learn."[43] Likewise, Jen Gilbert's work in *Sexuality in School* reflects these same commitments and further adds to this conversation about the underlying tensions present in attempts to eradicate sexuality from education, as well as the anxieties attached to doing this work. Gilbert utilizes Derrida's concept of hospitality to illuminate the inherently disruptive nature of sexuality in education and therefore the necessary requirement that education work to unconditionally welcome, however imperfectly, those who resist its rules and assumptions about truth, knowledge, and human rights.[44] The introduction of strangeness, especially in the form of queerness, amounts to an important resistance to education's dependence on legibility and predictability and is thus a risk worth taking: "Passion is not only about sexual desire; it also characterizes the energetic desire for more learning, for finding new ideas, and helps bind together communities of inquiry." [45]

The significance of this introduction of a kind of strange, queer curiosity and desire also lies in its use to justify emphasis on pleasure as a constitutive element of sexual experience. Some, like Fine and McClellan, highlight the place of discourses of desire, or, more accurately, the lack thereof in sex education and in public schools in the United States more broadly. Reflecting on Fine's work from the 1980s that asserted the necessity of adequately addressing desire in sexuality education, Fine and McClelland argue decades later that not only has this not happened but also that this failure is having more drastic and widely felt effects on women.[46] Others, including Louisa Allen and Moira Carmody, posit that acknowledgment and inclusion of queerness within sex education depend upon the "re-conceptualization of the potential of pleasure in sexuality education. In particular, we identify the need for wedging open spaces for the possibility of ethical pleasures, in forms that are not heteronormatively pre-conceived or mandatory."[47] This also requires acknowledgment of the "sexual subject," Allen argues, which has been made all but impossible by the way schools define students as "children" despite also situating them as at least somewhat sexual insofar as they engage with sex education at all.[48] Again, this is the radical potential that introducing an expanded understanding of sexuality might bring about in education should it itself be welcomed. Cognizant of the many challenges facing this kind of education, however, Vanessa Cameron-Lewis and Allen argue that the pervasiveness of narratives of danger, and the fear they often explicitly aim to produce, within sex education must be met with an exploration of "the interrelatedness of pleasure and danger in sexual intimacy."[49] The concluding suggestions that represent a majority of this research assert that fundamental to any attempt at cultivating these discourses is the need for student-centered approaches, which, as Nancy Kendall has described, are ones that allow for debate and deliberation over the issues, questions, and experiences that are most relevant to students' lives.[50]

Despite the import of these critiques, they can be read as limited specifically because, even when critiquing liberalism, they overwhelmingly leave the liberal state intact. At stake here is the power of recognizing and understanding the extent to which liberalism has historically and still is ideologically one of the most powerful mechanisms through which marginalization and exclusion are produced. This point has been made across many disciplines and for many reasons; however, its ability to permeate educational scholarship more broadly has remained weak. Though I could speculate as to why that might be, what is most relevant here is that there is a fundamental contradiction in relying on an institution that, by definition, creates patterns of inclusion and thus also exclusion that has been, up until this point, primarily utilized for the purpose of maintaining biopolitical boundaries between citizens and noncitizens, those deserving of rights and those not so deserving, and, in many ways, life deserving of life and life deserving of something less than life. Related to the problem of liberalism's insidious framing of sex education discourses is the general lack of structural analysis in the attempt to make sex education more inclusive within a liberal state. Not only does this liberal framework go unquestioned, but its relationship to violence also remains unquestioned in the move toward inclusion. The purpose of this project is therefore, in part, to demonstrate the dangers in leaving this framework unquestioned, and how those dangers are also unevenly distributed, particularly as they perpetuate colonial, racist, and capitalist logics. In neglecting a structural analysis, these connections go untheorized and, as a result, are left free to operate as they did—there is no mitigating mechanism put in place to address, let alone eradicate, these systematic and structural interdependencies, a cost that is felt by some much more than others.

Further, given what has been said thus far about sex education's relationship to colonialism, racism, and capitalism, it is clear that there are issues to be raised about the inability to maintain distance from state. When these critiques aim at inclusion or expansion of categories and content, then, they serve only to adjust the distance between what is good rational thought and behavior and irrational thought and behavior, moving those figures of diverse sexual identity into the realm of what constitutes good, valuable ways of thinking and being. Inclusion may expand that realm and decrease the realm of what constitutes bad ways of thinking and being, and it may even change how those realms are understood and described, but it does not in and of itself challenge the hierarchy underlying such adjudications of human value, nor does it end the processes of stigmatization and violences connected to it. This is the key lesson of intersectionality for sex education, then: in revealing the intricate and complicated relationship sex education has to violence, historically and ideologically, it helps us see the ways in which the language of inclusion and expansion fails to address the structures normalizing this violence. These authors of course *do* open up space for theorizing sex education differently, and this project reflects the fecund nature of that space. Again, I do not mean to suggest that any of these authors *intend* any kind of violence. My interest and concern lie instead with the desire to see more intentionality in how the category of the human is used in these spaces, as well as to see such intentionality as a way of both deepening the practice of destabilization that these scholars have helped to cultivate and working toward something more explicitly destructive.

While each contribution to this literature certainly *could* intervene upon the epistemological assumptions that define the "human" in such violent ways, my skepticism and concern related to the efficacy of them for doing so relates primarily to their dependence upon the state itself. Taken together, this body of scholarship almost completely hinges on arguments based on expansion and inclusion and, in the process, can be understood as attending more to a desire to move the dividing line between stigmatization and marginalization on the one hand, and respectability and state-centered recognition on the other. In privileging this approach to improving sex education in schools in the United States, these arguments overwhelmingly leave unaddressed the concept of the human that is desired in sex education, particularly as it relates to exploring the problematic closeness between reason, rationality, and intelligence and racism, capitalism and neoliberalism, colonialism, and, of course, state violence. To use the analogy of the ever-reliable weed, we might say that while these scholars do indeed help weed the garden, its roots remain and, as it turns out, the weed becomes more fickle and intelligent despite the weeding, learning how to survive in even the strangest of places. The conditions that produce the problems that are supposedly addressed remain themselves undisturbed, if not even more powerful. As one sex worker told an interviewer from the Urban Institute Report on the "underground commercial sex economy" in major cities in the United States, "A girl is never forced."[51]

4

The International Implications of Domestic Sex Education Policy

All forms of state violence have implications across borders, especially insofar as subjective straightening around nationalist norms impacts foreign relations. For this reason, I turn now to a consideration of the way sex education is situated in relation to the United States' own situatedness within global economies and politics. Up until this point, this project has largely been concerned with how the United States positions sex education at the federal level and its biopolitical impact on those subjects living within its borders, but its own domestic policies nonetheless implicate its foreign relations, too, and this chapter aims to begin a conversation around the nature and quality of this process. The United States' use of sex education as a form of state violence, I will argue, suggests something important about the status of sex education, and its future as a site of liberation, around the world: it cultivates subjects that are seen as inherently in need of protection *everywhere*, thus legitimizing the use of violence around the world as not just necessary, but even progressive, advanced, and democratic. Further, it devastates in the process by also cultivating subjects who are depicted as deserving their criminalization, often to deadly ends. As sex worker Kanyia Walker writes for the ACLU,

> A lot of us choose to get into sex work because the money is good and it is an environment where we can surround ourselves with other trans people. But some of us just don't have any other options because of discrimination in the legal job market. . . . We cannot survive and thrive if our lives are policed and criminalized.[1]

This chapter, therefore, centers the relationship between sexual subject formation domestically and sexual subject formation internationally by exploring three "global points of exchange" that allow for the exchange of ideologies across national borders: (1) policy—or an exploration of national sex education policies themselves; (2) the capitalist political economy—or a consideration of some of the economic practices that align sexual subjectivity with neoliberal aims; and (3) sexual labor trades themselves—or the production of a borderless industry of sexual labor, each with its own pedagogical lesson for us. In doing this, I hope to offer a reinterpretation of federal sex education policy in the United States as participating in violence well beyond its own political borders. The lessons here call for a need to come to terms with the nonviable separation between sex work and sex education to which the United States desperately clings.

State Violence Both Ways

The previous chapter briefly outlined how sex education enacts and bolsters certain forms of state violence that mark its own complicity in and with such violence, with a concentration on the way these processes and systems function within the permeable and politicized borders of the United States. There are, however, many important reasons for extending this understanding of the relationship between sex education and state violence to include global, transnational relations. The intimacy with which the United States positions its foreign affairs alongside the control of its own population has been essential to its development. Particularly after 9/11, the relationship between national security, terrorism, and domestic policing has been increasingly tightened and, at the same time, normalized, so as to make these phenomena almost indistinguishable and interchangeable within everyday political life. Manipulating racialized sexuality has always been inherent to these processes and continues to be as the relationship between the United States' domestic and foreign policies has become more closely aligned under global capitalism. Alimahomed-Wilson and Williams argue that "the privatization of state violence has become a driving force in today's global economy," such that not only does global capitalism change how social control is achieved domestically, but that such control itself fuels the insidiousness of capitalism and neoliberalism's reach across the world.[2] If federal sex education policies participate in and drive the extension of state violence into schools, acting as a site of normative subjectification that upholds racist and sexist conceptions of sexuality, gender, and the family, then its relationship to international politics is also in need of consideration. How do sex education's ties to state violence implicate it as part of the United States' global presence?

Again, there is a long history in the United States of crafting the citizen-subject in a way that aligns with foreign interests, especially related to "promoting democracy," preemptive war or war-like attacks, and intervention into other nations' government and wars. That is, the requirements for both citizenship and humanity within the United States' jurisdiction often cohere so as to create the very population that is righteously worth protecting in the face of variously defined threats. What is enacted through policy, legislation, or law within US borders, then, is also itself guided by the desire to cultivate something, or a population that is, morally defensible. In many cases, if not all, it is violence that is produced by this work: the citizen-subject that policy, legislation, and law are developed to cultivate is promised only through policing, surveillance, control, and criminalization, and, at the same time, the promise of such a cultivation is itself justification for protecting that subject from foreign powers, specifically by extending state violence across borders and foreign-ism within them.

Few aspects of human life exemplify these processes than do those that relate to racialization and sexualization. In *Freedom with Violence*, Reddy details how, central to the development of concepts of race, gender, and sexuality in the United States, especially during the twentieth century, was the process of attaching access to rights and recognition to policies and practices that legitimized and carried out the dehumanization of others. Reddy, in paying careful attention to the way the policing of sexuality and race happened during this period of US history, explains how the policing of identity and subjectification was regularly justified through the promise of specific forms of freedom. His analytic for understanding this paradox of freedom and violence, "freedom with violence," traces the way liberalism has historically operated to provide a kind of "bourgeois freedom" to disguise its commitments to logics that I have argued are central to state violence in the United States: white, patriarchal supremacy, racism, colonialism, and capitalism.[3] On this account, these logics also cohere with a narrowed view of what constitutes reason and rationality, as Reddy shows how the desire for such a freedom was framed and presented as rational and directly in opposition to the nonrational other who, at this point, is positioned by the state as all but asking to be treated violently.[4]

In short, the United States' depiction of citizen-subjectivity, exemplified by its development within sex education policy, might be seen as one of its greatest biopolitical resources (besides its capital, at least), which is used to impact policies of all kinds around the world in many different ways. The rest of this chapter is dedicated to exploring three of them.

Global Points of Exchange

Though there are likely many additional ways to think about the relationship between sexual subjectivity as it occurs domestically and internationally, the three I have chosen to explore here are especially relevant to considerations of the role of sex education in perpetuating violence against sex workers. In order to capture the borderlessness of these relationships, as well as to emphasize the transactional nature of them, I discuss the impact of United States' own domestic policies regarding sex education on sex education policies elsewhere in terms of "global points of exchange." These "points" represent moments of ideological transmission that facilitate the alignment of sexual subjectivity with state desires, particularly around erasing all discussions of sex work from sex education. I recognize the instability and fluidity of these ideas and practice categorization only for the sake of analytic clarity. The points of ideological transmission I will discuss are (1) policies around sex education and sex work; (2) interconnectedness via involvement in the global capitalist economy; and (3) the status of sex work itself.

Policy Exchanges

Federal sex education policies in the United States have had inconsistent impacts on national sex education policies in other countries, though the reverse is also true, if not somewhat less significantly so. Whereas some country's policies might be seen as being pulled more *into* the United States' framework for approaching sexual subjectivity in schools, some can be seen as pushing *away* from its proposed norms. As a result, some have crafted sex education policies that either only take the more progressive aims of comprehensive sex education policy proposals seriously or simply offer different programs by virtue of their distinct historical contexts. A project this size cannot account for all sex education policies everywhere, so I have chosen to explore three nations that offer a glimpse into the exchanges around sexual subjectivity and the lessons these exchanges offer for our considerations of violence. The nations are China, Nigeria, and Brazil. In each case, the impact of sex education policy discourses from the United States is clearly displayed, the existence of sex work is of national concern, and the former remains generally unconcerned with the latter. While in each case there are differences derived from each nation's own relationships to capitalism, colonialism, and the United States itself, as well as different understandings of the implications of sexual normativity for the development of the nation-state, the general dissonance between the status of sex work and workers and the aims of sex education is what is most important to this project.

I have purposefully left out an especially important set of Western countries in making these choices, however. These include Canada, Sweden, the Netherlands, Finland, Spain, Germany, Australia, and Switzerland, to name a few. I want to acknowledge the essential work on sex education, both academic and otherwise, in and about these nations, as well as the many ways in which these nation's policies have been informed by the institutionalized practices of sex education in the United States. Many of these nations also represent rich spaces for exploring what is possible outside of the context of the United States, especially given the far more "progressive" nature of many of these nation's policies on sex work (it is legal, at least in part, in each of the countries I just listed). In making this choice, I do *not* mean to suggest that there is less to say, or fewer important things to say, about these global relations. What I *do* mean to suggest, however, is that there are other nations, ones often left out of Western-centric debates over how sexual subjectification plays out in educational spaces, for which these relations are quite different and especially informative given the concerns with violence at stake in this project. There is so much work to be done within this space, and I know that what is offered here barely scratches that surface.

One thing that China, Nigeria, and Brazil all have in common as it relates to sex education is that their national policies, no matter how contentious, are derived from or measured internally according to the UNESCO standards for comprehensive sex education. First introduced in 2009, UNESCO offered "technical guidance" "to assist education policy matters in all countries design accurate and age-appropriate curricula for children and young people aged

5-18+."⁵ Guided by what UNESCO director-general Audrey Azoulay describes as a human rights and gender equality framework, these guidelines now center comprehensive sexuality education in order to disseminate information about "the physical, social and emotional challenges" youth face during puberty, and to "tackle" issues of access to "contraception, early pregnancy, gender-based violence, sexually transmitted infections (STIs) and HIV and AIDS." Further, these guidelines emphasize the importance of intervening in the spread of HIV and AIDS and also the explicit importance of addressing "the large body of material of variable quality that young people find on the internet, and help them face increasingly common instances of cyberbullying." These guidelines were updated in 2018, funded in large part by Sweden and UNAIDS. In the section titled, "The Evidence Base for Comprehensive Sexuality Education," UNESCO describes its sources of information as consisting of two reviews: one done by Douglas Kirby and another review of research done by two researchers from the University of Oxford Center for Evidence-Based Intervention.

Dr. Kirby is considered one of the most important researchers on sex education of the past fifty years. The research that has been most influential is that which he has done on birthrates, age of sexual initiation, HIV/AIDs, teen pregnancy, and condom use, research which was directly called upon in the creation of Obama's Teen Pregnancy Prevention Initiative and PREP program, discussed earlier. Personally, my engagement with Kirby's work has led to an appreciation of the consistent *ambivalence* he derived from his research. That his findings have been so globally implemented has led to a tendency to erase what is more complicated about them: that the impact of most comprehensive sex education programs is not nearly as efficacious as he wanted it to be. Writing about Kirby's impact on the field of sex education around the work, Leslie Kantor and colleagues describe some of Kirby's own frustrations with his research findings and detail the fact that much of his research found *weaknesses* in programs, *not* strengths.⁶ Though he worked hard to translate his findings into programs that might address these weaknesses, it is important to note that it was his own suggestions for such improvement that "changed the field" of sex education and not the success of those suggestions. This is important because, given that UNESCO relies so much on (though not exclusively) one American researcher, as having been essential in upholding the very standards that I am arguing ought to be challenged, the proliferation of these logics throughout the world itself ought to be challenged, too. This research and these measures of success, and the values they aim at, are not themselves unworthy, and the project of addressing a pandemic like HIV/AIDS should not be underappreciated. What I worry about is that in disseminating this framework, which uses conclusions derived largely from the context of the United States, there has also been dissemination of the normative assumptions about the human that the United States also depends upon. More specifically, in each of the countries discussed here, these guidelines shape contemporary debates around the purpose and necessity of comprehensive sex education while also fundamentally ignoring those who are most likely to be impacted by the problems it claims to address: sex workers.

Very recently—in October of 2020; set to go into effect in June of 2021—the National People's Congress Standing Committee of the People's Republic of China announced the implementation of "age-appropriate sex education for minors," again based on UNESCO's guidelines. As in the United States, though, the status of a national policy for sex education in China is contentious. In China, one of the reasons for these contentions is related to its communist past, especially Chairman Mao's commitment to the necessity of regulating sexuality for the sake of social harmony.[7] Another reason is because of its own history with eugenics. In her account of the history of sex education in China for the past century, Alessandra Aresu writes about how the "origins" of national discussions about sex education within the area of Chinese control themselves date back to the early 1900s. She further discusses how the idea of sex education at this time was seen as a "catchall" term for anything that worked to "regulate sexual activities" including those that aimed to "keep sexual relations within the monogamous marital couple," "the elimination of premarital and extramarital sex," promote "premarital chastity," and eliminate "'evil habits' and practices, such as masturbation, prostitution and sodomy," with extra emphasis on the "social evil" and "source of contamination" that was prostitution.[8] As in the United States, these aims were deeply connected to eugenicist concerns with creating a strong, moral society. However, again, there are important breaks in this shared discourse, even despite the reliance upon UNESCO's guidelines. For example, a member of UNESCO Beijing, Li Hongyan, has acknowledged that there is likely to be backlash to these policies specifically because of the attitude of concern for what "could be seen as promoting individuality" in the country.[9] As it relates to eugenics, though it has recently been rescinded, China's "one-child" policy has shaped discourse around the implementation of a national sex education curriculum profoundly. Despite the fact that there remains a heated debate around how successful the policy was in controlling population growth, there is concern about how successful the termination of the policy will be in changing people's behaviors given its power as a discourse for understanding family and reproductive issues in the country. This is especially the case given that China still has the second largest number of adolescents in the world, with approximately 230 million citizens between the age of ten and twenty-four.[10] In this way, UNESCO's Western-oriented projection of what constitutes "sexual education" remains at some odds with Chinese culture, though the push for comprehensive sex education continues, often on the very basis that China ought to modernize its curriculum.

In Nigeria, the issue of sex education is embedded within a different set of concerns, though still advocated for based on UNESCO guidelines. In 1999 the Nigerian government approved sexuality education as a national project and has continued to wrestle with what it should look like. Shiffman et al., however, have shown how insidious the impact of "international norms" has been on the country. They write that "Sexuality education in Nigeria represents, prima facie, a hard case for theories claiming strong influence of international norms of national policy-making."[11] Taking into consideration the influence of religion in Nigeria—primarily Christianity and Islam—they show that, despite this, the presence of NGOs in Nigeria beginning in the 1980s and the influx of international donors were essential in the national government taking on the project of sex education and have continued to bolster a growing population of "domestic champions" of sex education. Also notable is the impact of an encounter between a Nigerian advocate for sex education and a speaker from the Sexuality Information and Education Council of the United States (SIECUS) in the early 1990s. Shiffman et al. describe the impact of this meeting in the following way:

> She subsequently initiated a process that led to the development of Nigerian guidelines. With funding and technical support from SIECUS, and additional funding from the MacArthur Foundation, she organized the National Guidelines Task Force in 1995, which included NGOs, medical associations, UN agencies, officials from the Federal Ministries of Education and Health, researchers, media and religious representatives. Many had been working independently on adolescent reproductive health. This was the first explicit

effort in the country to build a policy community surrounding sexuality education.[12]

If the controversy over sex education today has had any impact on this national curriculum, it has been in making consistency and thoroughness of the curriculum almost impossible to implement. These debates often center the very concern for "Western imposition" that is reflected in Chinese discourse on the necessity of a national comprehensive sex education program and again suggests that this imposition, ideologically grounded in the values asserted by the US government and other American institutions, has had a profound influence in shaping what constitutes a legitimate way of life in Nigeria.

In Brazil, the debates around a national sex education curriculum revolve around a different American ideal: abstinence. In large part due to the dominance of Catholic values in the country, and, most recently, driven by Brazil's president, Jair Bolsonaro, sex education in Brazil has been consistently diluted in recent years. Though not perfect, the policies of sex education prior to Bolsonaro and the increased power of religious conservatism over the past decade are missed by many. The undermining of sex education is often blamed on a series of events beginning in 2010, wherein former president Dilma Rousseff halted the distribution of sex education materials in Brazilian schools. The materials most at issue were what are referred to as "anti-homophobia kits," which were condemned by evangelical Christian groups that threatened political backlash should these materials make it into children's hands.[13] This was a pivotal moment in securing conservative power in the discussion around sex education in the nation. Despite ample pushback from Brazilian organizations supporting comprehensive sex education, again utilizing the standards set by UNESCO, the national government has consistently rejected these recommendations and maintains the value of abstinence education as the only decent path forward as a nation.[14] Nearly ten years later, in 2019, it was reported that Bolsonaro would support national legislation to cut back on funding for, and limit the influence of, sex education across the country, a move that eight cities took on their own in the years between Rousseff's actions on sex education and Bolsonaro's own announcement.[15] Bolsonaro and his administration have continually repeated common American refrains around abstinence since. For example, in 2020, the minister of human rights, family, and women, Damares Alves, announced the government's allegiance to a new campaign, "I Chose to Wait," and said, "Our young people, by and large, are having sex as a result of social pressure. You can go to a party and have lots of fun without having sex."[16] That this language directly parallels that of abstinence in the United States is no accident.

There are more lessons to be gleaned from this short consideration of the relationship between national policies and their own import for understanding systems of institutionalized violence across borders than what I will highlight here, though I certainly hope to be part of this research in the future. This is especially important to me because there is very little, if anything, that offers a comparative analysis of sex education policy's between nations in this way, and I believe that there is inherent value for doing this work, especially as we face an increasingly globalized and neoliberal political economy that will inevitably remain dependent upon the regulation of sex, gender, and sexuality for its own sustenance.[17] Here, however, I will simply offer two tentative conclusions as they relate to this project. First, what is most striking to me in exploring these connections are the ways in which those logics that frame what is considered by many in the United States to be the *least* desirable kinds of sex education remain at play and even of value in different nations on different continents around the world. Despite any critiques of the concepts of abstinence, moralizing about female sexuality, reliance upon human tropes that justify racist or xenophobic lessons and practices, and even the relationship to capitalism that are prominent within discourse on sex education in the United States, it seems to be that the most profound impact these discourses have had in other nations is *not* the bringing to bear of those critiques but the *preservation* of those ideologies, and the biopolitical distinctions between whose lives matter and whose do not that they maintain, themselves.

Beyond this, though, is the stark reality that is revealed when these ideologies are considered alongside the fact that in every country discussed here, sex work is on the rise and sex workers are organizing to gain rights based on assertions of the validity of their existence and the legitimacy of their labor. In China, while sex work remains officially illegal, it is thriving and becoming more desirable, specifically because of the dominance of factory work in job creation, which is either unappealing or insufficient for many young women today. Sex workers in China are therefore also constructing meaningful kinship networks to support each other as the state continues to stigmatize and criminalize them. In many ways, then, sex work is essential to the survival of significant portions of the population. For example, in her research on sex workers in China, Yeon Jung Yu highlights the emergence of moral systems used by sex workers in Hainan Island to argue that, given the pressures put on young people to support their families, the value of sex work is largely underappreciated and misunderstood. In reflecting upon the "apparent contradictions" within the moral codes structuring the relationships between sex workers, she writes, "These are not really contradictions—they are sensible components of a morality that is specific to this community . . . the women I lived with were, on the contrary, highly concerned with upholding their moral code."[18] In this way, sex work provides these women with an essential social network that allows for more consistent income and more financial stability than can often otherwise be attained, both of which are of course essential in a capitalist world.

Additionally, in Nigeria, where sex work is also technically illegal, there has been in development a thriving sex work community that has also begun to organize to advance their rights. The Nigeria Sex Workers Association, colloquially known as the Precious Jewels, has as its mission: "to empower and strengthen the voices of sex workers, advocate for their health, social and human rights including those living with HIV and those using drugs, through collaborations, networking and partnerships."[19] Also, in 2019, a High Court in Nigeria ruled that sex work was not punishable by the law. Similarly, in Brazil, sex workers are organizing and making strides in demanding rights and protections, even at their own peril. The marginalization and criminalization sex workers face in Brazil have been exacerbated by the anti-LGBTQ practices and beliefs that circulate the national government, and the consequences have been devastating, with the murder of LGBTQ sex workers, especially trans sex workers, becoming, as in the United States, a regular occurrence. In preparation for the 2016 Trans Day of Visibility, it was reported by Transgender Europe that the murder rate for trans people in Brazil was the highest in the world, suggesting that what happens to sex workers is a reflection of the environment around sexuality at large.[20] Despite this, because of the status of poor non-Western women around the world, sex work in Brazil is similarly considered by sex workers as essential to survival and appealing given the lack of sufficient alternatives for securing income. In *The Conversation*, Amanda De Lisio and Michael Silk quote one woman involved in sex work in Brazil as describing her relationship with her peers as one of a "family," and a family that helps make sure her own "real" family is cared for:

"I work today to give my children a better future, not to leave my daughter in public school. Healthcare is the same. I pay for education and health insurance otherwise my daughter would be without them."[21] In each of these countries, sex work is both essential *and* remains a site of tremendous gender-, race-, and sexuality-based violence. That these sex education policies continue to erase the experiences of sex workers as part of the imagined community for which it claims to provide support and education mirrors the erasures that the United States depends upon in maintaining its own legitimacy as a system for sexual straightening. The absence of attention within sex education policies that claim to care about citizen's health and well-being to those most deserving of attention both reproduces the very erasure that the United States' own sex education policies have cultivated and creates and normalizes an illusion of care that might instead be understood as violence.

I want to be extremely clear about one thing, here, given the predominance of concerns about "exploitation" and trafficking that circulate educational spaces: my discussion of the experience of sex workers should *not* be understood as making a generalizable normative evaluation of sex work, nor am I making a claim that the violence facing sex workers is going to be addressed adequately or even inherently well by guidance from sex worker movements. I think it is all far more complicated than this, and there are many ways in which taking a firm stand on the moral nature of sex work would inevitably be a certain kind of neocolonial feminist argument itself in this case, given my own position as a cis-female White academic in the United States. The normative point I am making here is about the facade of concern put on by sex education policies, even comprehensive ones. If we care about our communities, this care must always include even the most marginalized, and this always includes sex workers; instead, sex education continues to marginalize sex work and sex workers to the point of erasure. This *is* its biopolitical purpose. Any concern for addressing violence must attend to this gap in consideration for who constitutes the "community." It says something about the nature of the violence that I am arguing is present within US federal sex education policy and reflected in other nations across the world, that, no matter how little it is funded, no matter how thoroughly it is critiqued, the erasures produced in the United States are produced through its dominance in defining what constitutes "good" sex education in other nations. Second, though, exploring federal sex education policies in this way suggests its role in globalization itself. It is not new to point to the way US policies and practices do this in general, but it is new to see sex education as part of this phenomenon and to consider what this means for attempts to save or shift the very project of sex education itself. It matters that the discourses circulated in federal policy here shape discourses elsewhere and that, together, they sustain, if not everywhere then at least in many *somewheres*, the very forms of biopolitical violence that those concerned with aligning sex education with nonviolent purposes and aims claim to disavow.

Systemic Interconnectedness within the Global Capitalist Economy

Federal sex education policies also have an explicit interest in defending particular kinds of kinship formations and sexual relations. As was most developed in the previous chapter, the standard for normalcy, that is the nuclear family itself, normalizes punishing those who do not meet this standard. While the United States has a seeming "two steps forward, one step back" approach to expanding rights and protections to those who fail in this way, the "forward"-ness of the narrative around racialized sexuality and sexual relationships reveals the progress narrative embedded within this normalizing quality of sex education policy. The Progressive era's commitment to the defense of American progress becomes, in more recent policies, a commitment to modeling this progress for the rest of the world. Contradictorily, forward progress, as defined in US policy, is interpreted as a call to "bring" progress elsewhere and to intervene where progress is being stunted. Jasbir Puar's work, for example, details how the extension of rights to gay and lesbian subjects in the United States has resulted in "homonationalism," an ideological investment asserting the normative value of being a "gay-friendly" nation as a legitimate justification for foreign intervention and violence. She writes, "[Homonationalism] is rather a facet of modernity and a historical shift marked by the entrance of (some) homosexual bodies as worthy of projection by nation-states, a constitutive and fundamental reorientation of the relationship between the state, capitalism, and sexuality." This projection of its own progress onto foreign affairs creates a "narrative of progress for gay rights [that is] built on the back of racialized others, for whom such progress was once achieved, but is now backsliding or has yet to arrive."[22]

Further, Puar connects the stakes of this progress narrative to neoliberalism and its own ableist requirements by asking, "Which bodies are made to pay for 'progress'? Which debilitated bodies can be reinvigorated for neoliberalism, and which cannot?"[23] This question, I think, may as well be understood as the quintessence of federal sex education's violence: as demonstrated in many recent events, the cost of inclusion is allowing oneself to be judged on the basis of economic performance, and, too, being a citational reference for the need for foreign presence and violence. Puar points to the torture at Abu Ghraib in the 2000s as exemplifying this, but I would add that the continued presence and influence of the United States in the Middle East, the Philippines, and Central America is in each case at least partially justified by the seemingly unquestionable interest in "protecting" women (and children) and queer people from "dangerous" "regimes." On this, even, or perhaps especially, when couched in language around feminism, M. Jacqui Alexander, among others, notes that Western feminism's relationship to progressivism often causes a similar "paradoxical gesture of flattening out and assimilating difference on the one hand, while freezing and reifying it on the other" when it attempts to evaluate conditions of inequity and inequality by its own standards elsewhere. [24]

The previous chapters also detailed the relationship between federal sex education policies in the United States and the criminalization of nonnormative subjects and experiences domestically. The quality and consequences of criminality assigned and honed by such policies to foreign subjects and experiences create a specific understanding of the internal "opponent" or "enemy" of the state and easily reduce those who appear as somehow foreign. On this, Mark Unger argues that the United States has a long history of casting LGBT individuals as "foreign agents," and I believe this quality remains in place today.[25] Again, homonationalism relates foreign-ness to normative failure, thus situating domestic federal policies on sexuality as *expanding* the category of criminality it imposes on its own inhabitants to those beyond the traditional legal jurisdiction of the US state. Likewise, given the pervasive concern within the United States around mass incarceration and its relationship to race, gender, and sexuality, it is telling that these so-called criminals are assigned foreign-like traits by white, capitalist society; they lose citizenship rights, labor rights, human rights, and agency in general. The concept of the criminal as it is produced within the United States creates a blueprint for what is to happen to those who betray its norms, sexual, citizen, or otherwise, and thus, despite the performance of homonationalism, also points to the hypocrisy of that performance itself.

Even though the phrase "family first" is commonly used to further what is now overwhelmingly bipartisan (even when it claims to be partisan) interest in preserving the nuclear family, thinking about this narrative in relationship to subjectivity and the blurred lines between domestic and foreign policy aims sheds new light on the way federal sex education policies participate in the creation and maintenance of the conditions under which the United States can explain away its presence in almost every corner of the globe. In a recent guest editorial in *Political Geography*, Smith et al. (2019) offer a response to the Trump administration's "zero-tolerance" policy of separating parents and children at the border between Mexico and the United States that has vital relevance to the issue of sex education policy. They argue that

> one way through which the (white) US nation-state is territorialized is the mechanism of denying childhood and kinship to racialized peoples in the name of "protecting" the white family. Performative apathy and cruelty enacts the border onto racialized bodies, excluding migrant children and families from the nation, and sanctions violence by naturalizing their subordination in a racial hierarchy.

I argue, following this, that federal sex education policy can be read as part of the United States' common practice of using the idealized, racialized, heteronormative family unit to reconstruct the boundaries of humanity maintained by the state today. These authors also argue that the denial of humanity as justified by the denial of kinship rights is connected to long-standing colonial practices of institutionalizing the right of the state to steal Native and Indigenous children from their own families. The denial of the legitimacy of slave's own family units and debates around the adoption rights for LGBTQ+ families are also examples of this continued practice. If we align this point with the concern for "innocence" that plagues contemporary sex education policy, "family-first" narratives that employ a narrow definition of the family against other forms of kinship also participate in in further laying the foundation for streamlining public discourse around national security and foreign threat with that which threatens the stability of the American family. The state's own fantasy about the inherent moral virtue and natural authenticity of the family founds its own delusions about global superiority and righteousness. If family is first, but only if it looks like a typical American one, then the side effects or consequences of defending it are necessary and justifiable, no matter how violent.

Lastly, in each case, there is an important relationship to democratic governance that ought to be reflected upon. While it is not central to this project, democracy is nonetheless implicated in each of these maneuvers made by sex education in relation to the United States' foreign policy agendas. The "promotion," "spreading," "bringing," "gifting," and "defending" of democracy by the United States, and in other nations, has been a long-standing goal of the government. Though it has been the subject of critique by academics and politicians, among others, for just as long, the assumed and often uncritical status of democracy as the ideal form of governance has, over and over again, justified anti-democratic practices. On this point, Mark Ungar poignantly shares that the attempt to "democratize" the world has actually "left many non-democratic practices intact. Amidst continuing political uncertainty and economic change, one of the practices many new democracies are either unable or unwilling to alter is state violence."[26]

Sex Work Industry

As with all other aspects of life on planet Earth, the nature of sex work has changed in the past century in ways that make its relationship to sex education different than I have argued it was in the early twentieth century. The implications of these changes are still emerging, and the meaning of them is always evolving, but those already doing the work of making sense of the current nature of sex work have convincingly challenged the stability of the category of sex work as reducible to prostitution and/or as inherently exploitative through their scholarly labor. As mentioned in the Introduction, the very definition of sex work has since been expanded largely as a result of the transformations caused by changes in technology, communication, and transportation that occurred in the twentieth century. As a result, scholars and activists generally understand sex work as a category of labor that includes the exchange of any and all kinds of pleasure and intimacy for any and all kinds of economic and/or material benefits.

In the United States alone, then, and in the same moment the federal government continues to invest in sex education programs that prioritize abstinence, monogamy, the family, and the resulting financial stability that is promised by the successful embodiment of these qualities, the industries around sex, sexuality, gender, and sex work, which cut across all races, classes, and abilities, are thriving. Sex education therefore helps to uphold these industries by ignoring them, as doing so creates the conditions under which any sexual activity ignored or erased also becomes desirable, whether that is because it is made to be taboo, "exotic," immoral, or merely illicit. Elizabeth Bernstein's careful analysis of the global sex work industry details this phenomenon as it occurs at a global level. She defines the global sex work industry as "a brave new world of commercially available intimate encounters that are subjectively normalized for sex workers and clients alike,"[27] and a "broadly encompassing designation for all forms of sexual labor."[28] As with the others, Bernstein highlights the privileging of prostitution as the ideal type of sex work as significant because it is one which allows for the playing out of moral disagreements most easily in public discourse.[29] However, prostitutes mark but one kind of work within this global force, and focus on prostitutes in particular hides the far reaching and powerful industry that is at work in the background of such activity:

> By all accounts, the sex industry has far exceeded its prior bounds to become a multifaceted, multibillion dollar industry, produced by and itself producing developments in other sectors of the global economy, such as hotel chains, tourism, long-distance telephone carriers, cable companies, and information technology, and creating burgeoning profits from right- and left-wing entrepreneurs alike.[30]

Any one of these industries could be explored more deeply in order to understand the relationship between the United States' policies that are criminalizing sex work and its commitment to violence within and beyond its borders. However for the sake of this project, and because of its powerful presence, I want to briefly explore the emergence of sex tourism.

The emergence of a global sex work market within tourist industries is, once again, a product of the merger between settler colonialism, capitalism, and racialized patriarchy. Sex tourism, defined by Wonders and Michalowski, is "a protean term that attempts to capture varieties of leisure travel that have as a part of their purpose the purchase of sexual services."[31] Writing about the "significant contributor" to tourism, that is sex tourism, Ros Williams, following the path set out by Fanon, argues that sexual relationships between colonizers and the colonized, across borders and classes and races and ethnicities, are part of colonial logics.[32] Williams shows that the global tourist industry has become dependent upon an "oppositional" relationship, inherent to colonialism, between the tourist and the "indigenous" population with which that tourist seeks contact.[33] Kamala Kempadoo's work on sex work in the Caribbean, for instance, highlights how colonization has shaped sex work in those islands. Her own work identifies the way in which an economy around sex and sexuality developed alongside the colonialist "pursuit of riches," which situated access to bodies and sex as essential to the establishment of colonial power.[34] Williams explains how this presumption of access became a profitable source for the tourism industry, especially the typical white, heterosexual, wealthy North American or European subject,[35] and profitable for sex workers that fulfill some aspect of the colonial imaginary of that tourist.

The modern industry of sex tourism also has its roots in a moment all too familiar to this project: the world wars. In fact, in her work on the global sex tourism industry, Jillian Grouchy directly asserts that the contemporary industry may have been born in the same moment as I have argued federal sex education policy to have been developed, writing that during these wars, soldiers "needed places to relax and recreate after a long walk and trajectories in camps," creating new markets for bars and brothels.[36] The recognition of this demand as a market demand, regardless of its appeal to the federal government, seems to have set the stage for using sex work to market certain spaces and locations and similarly associating deviancy with relaxation and pleasure. Grouchy notes, too, that the motivation for sex workers across the world still revolves around the idea that it "keeps them out of the poverty line," and "they create a livelihood from the industry," a narrative that mirrors the same expressions by prostitutes in the early twentieth century in the United States.[37] Sex tourism reflects, then, the neoliberal state's understanding that this industry can be itself a source of economic gain; the centrality of sex work to an industry that is otherwise advertised as one of the only ways to find relaxation and happiness points to the state's willingness to capitalize from the very industry it so often criminalizes.

The existence of this industry, and its presence around the world, suggests that despite any formal attempt at *ending* sex work in and by the United States, it has, in fact, only continued to thrive. Though sex education in a select few other nations has certainly come to reflect the popularity and pervasiveness of sex work, including the necessity of advocating for sex workers and the need for their labor to be decriminalized as part of other movements for social equity and justice, the United States continues to legislate in ways that only cause *harm* to sex workers by using such politics to make biopolitical determinations about acceptable ways of being. Most recently, this has been exemplified in the passing of the FOSTA-SESTA laws, which have quite successfully reduced all sex work to sex trafficking, further entrenching the industry and those who work in it in a discourse of theft, exploitation, and the decimation of innocence reminiscent of the "white slavery" discourse from over a century ago. The dissonance, both moral and cognitive, that the federal government continues to operate with is, therefore, telling in understanding its use of sex education as a tool for state violence.

In reflecting upon these tensions and contradictions and silences, it becomes evident that there is a way in which sex work and sex workers do as much, if not more, pedagogical work in our society than sex education. We learn from the way the United States and other nations handle sex work that the increasing visibility of those fighting to show the legitimacy of sex work and to defend sex workers' right to exist can only be met with narratives about violence, disease, and shame. However, if we do not buy into this, we learn something about sex education, too; even in its more comprehensive forms, it remains disconnected from the lives of millions around the world and, for this reason, continues to do more work to erase these millions than it does to address violence. It is also important to consider what is taught to us about sexual subjectivity given the fact that this erasure seems to *maintain* the industry of sex work—it makes it more taboo, more enticing, more profitable, and more interesting. In this way, sex education helps make the very conditions of its existence necessary.

Illusive Erasures and Their Lessons

How do we reconcile these global patterns and practices alongside policies like the ones for sex education in which the United States continues to invest and reinvest? More than mere hypocrisy, there seems to be value for the state in maintaining this stark pedagogical discrepancy. That is, there are lessons to be learned in reflecting upon the presence of this dissonance.

First, the *nationalism*, or demand for national subject formation, inherent to federal sex education policy, erases the floundering nature of political land borders themselves within an ever-more-present *global capitalist structure*. In this erasure, or in maintaining strict boundaries between "here" and "there," "us" and "them," sex education ignores the extent to which it is precisely sex and sexuality that have been central to the rise of capitalism, the emergence of neoliberalism, and the rise of global capitalism as arguably the most dominant political force at this moment in history. The United States' imperial desires also rest upon these discourses around sex and sexuality. However, a "truth" the emergence of this sex tourism industry reveals is that the possibility of empire is undermined by global capitalism; the tensions between nation building and capitalism are at play, then, in sex education, insofar as the refusal to admit to its deep, inextricable relationship to capitalism may lie in a fear of, or confusion around, the declining ability for any one nation to maintain distinct global authority and power.

Second, the demand for *sexual normativity* creates an industry around *deviancy* that is profitable to the very people who demand deviancy be eradicated. The example of marriage is useful here. While marriage is idealized in sex education, it is often precisely the instability of the institution that makes sex work so appealing to so many, from all perspectives. It is also telling that the difference between sex work and marriage is, on many accounts, not all that clear itself. Even federal sex education policies reveal this. Emma Goldman, Gayle Rubin, and many since them have also argued that marriage is fundamentally a form of economic exchange and labor; following this, sex education supports one form of sex work while demonizing another, a move that is almost invisible because of, and also further sustained by, the moralism implicit to its economic concerns. In noting this, I do not mean to flatten all sex work into one common experience, and it is also not the case that the issues surrounding sex work are the same across countries. What I do mean to do is to identify the industry of sex work as powerful in shaping sexual subjectivity, making the demands for sexual normativity posited in sex education policies across the world antithetical and even laughable to a growing number of people and their lives. Further, if sex education cannot talk about sex work, this dissonance is only likely to grow, which could either destabilize the narratives that attempt to legitimize sex education or force sex education to acknowledge what it has been trying to do all along: eradicate sex work. Or, it could do both.

Third, and perhaps most important, late capitalism and its desire to profit from every aspect of existence has its own imperial nature, and the federal public education system in the United States, along with all other public institutions, remains caught in a battle over the purpose of politics and government itself that this creeping globalism causes: Is the role of government to protect *life* or to protect *profit*? This is an epistemological question just as much as it is a political or economic one. That is, at stake in this question is also a concern for how the ideas of "education," "rationality," "reason," and "intelligence" will be defined, as are the very criteria upon which moral determinations will be made. The erasure of this tension within sex education policy serves as a reminder of the depths of this problem throughout all of education itself and gives us an answer to the question—can sex education policy reform resist state violence?—that motivated this project to begin with: almost certainly not.

It could be helpful to think about these erasures in terms of anxiety. For how long can these contradictions and erasures last, or for how long will the illusions they provide persist in the desired ways? Can neoliberalism successfully erase the presence of any kind of resistance to the naturalization of capitalist determinations of moral goodness? Or will the concept of education, somehow, become too antagonistic to its aims? And isn't this why sex education, and any real significant structural changes to it, is so terrifying to both the state and its subjects? Despite my critiques of contemporary sex education scholarship, one point from them rings true here: sexuality is what cannot be predicted and cannot be controlled; it cannot be detached from the sensuous desire for more, from what is exciting and life altering and impossible, and it certainly cannot be fully constrained by neoliberalism. To allow for sexuality in its fullness to exist in education is to invite in the biggest threat there is to education's own ability to exist itself: those whose existence is proof of its destructive nature. Doing this makes education vulnerable to its own undoing and reveals its complicity in the very biopolitical straightening that sex education makes possible. So, what do we do?

In closing this chapter, I want to add that there is a cruelty to always only chopping away at the worst of what we can see. And yet, somehow, like Sisyphus, we continue to push this bolder up the hill. And it is perhaps because, as Camus famously argues, Sisyphus's mythical representation often romanticizes the meaninglessness attached to this way of life, that we ourselves keep assuming that contentment can be found in the process. So long as love, of the other, of the family, of the country, remains the political North Star of sex education reform, the only hope we can have for the future is that it will be a place where more people can experience the love some have found in these idealized forms of kinship and reproduction.

This cruelty is reminiscent of what Lauren Berlant calls "cruel optimism." Berlant writes that objects of desire are really "clusters of promises" that only optimism about those promises can sustain.[38] But, when the promises are either destine to be broken, or if the optimism that is attached to those promises is "sheer fantasy, or *too* possible, and toxic," the optimism is a cruel one.[39] She adds,

> What's cruel about these attachments, and not merely inconvenient or tragic, is that the subjects who have *x* in their lives might well not endure the loss of their object or scene of desire, even though its presence threatens their well-being; because whatever the *content* of the attachment is, the continuity of the form of it provides something of the continuity of the subject's sense of what it means to keep on living on and look forward to being in the world.[40]

In the next chapter, then, it is the cruelty of maintaining an optimism around the idea of sex education that is interrogated. It is the cruelty of remaining hopeful about an institution that refuses education for and about those who, in their own words, are "smart and curious," who "like to learn about ourselves, our community, and the world around us," that motivates the demand for something else.[41]

5

Alternatives, Not Adjustments; Imagination, Not Intervention

Acknowledging the way that sex education facilitates the seeping and spreading of violence across spaces, borders, and lives necessarily demands the imagining of alternative intervening possibilities. As Margo St. James once said, "what my goal is, is the complete decriminalization of sex for human beings, even commercial sex."[1] The future of sex education is, therefore, implicated by this demand, given its role in this violence. In this chapter, I explore the limits of advocating for new state-sponsored *policies* in bringing about different, nonviolent futures, and instead argue for the cultivation of alternative, imaginative, sexual *pedagogies*. It is only through the development and use of such pedagogies, when they are grounded in ways of knowing and being that challenge the intricate relationship between sexuality, race, capital, labor, and knowledge that we might begin to address the insidious ways in which sex education, as a federally funded institution, perpetuates violence. Considering this, then, what might education do with sexuality?

This chapter ultimately offers an argument for ending sex education as it currently exists. Despite being a regular target of neoliberal policy frustrations that demand immediate "action," I understand critique as essential to the possibility of any kind of liberatory praxis and as an act itself.[2] As such, I offer this critique by homing in on common educational refrains about policy, progress, and imagination that enact powerful limits to radical imaginative processes. Following this, I offer what is merely meant to serve as an example of how one *might* proceed, or a provocation for something different, given the understanding of federal sex education policy detailed throughout this book, and, therefore, *not* a requirement, a demand, or any kind of prescriptive dictate about what should be done next. Though the project thus far has already had a connection to imagination, I aim to use this space to experiment with imaginings that culminate in a simple proposal: that we try something else. In fact, I am deeply reluctant to suggest in any way that I can or should imagine *for* others; instead, because of my commitment to opening possibilities, I resist the likely call to explain with any kind of normative specificity what should follow this. Doing so would foreclose the very possibilities that I also humbly imagine to be out there, somewhere else, waiting to be called into existence by others. What is offered here may spark something new or different in the reader that itself alters their presence in the world and their praxis toward liberation and justice, or, of course, it may not. The possibilities are truly always evolving and infinitely developing, so this chapter ought to be read as nothing other than an attempt to legibly articulate my own feelings and understandings that lead me to desire very different and novel possibilities for what education might look like, sound like, and feel like.

In what follows, then, I offer a critique of policy reform, with a view into the value of pedagogical interventions into the relationship between sexuality and education in schools. Next, I call upon debates in education and beyond regarding the radical possibilities inherent to the cultivation and practice of imagination in order to detail the potential in letting imagination guide pedagogical theorizing and practice. Given imagination's relationship to utopian thought and hope, I offer a discussion of the resistance to optimism, or optimistic hope, within discourses on queer futurity and think through the value of creating space for a different kind of hope, grounded in "negative" affect and even apathy, to suggest the latent, rich possibilities inherent to walking away from sex education. In opposition against, and even defiance of, the pressure to outline "practical" and "productive" paths toward change, I will purposefully rest in the much more ambiguous space of what I refuse to accept.

Against Policy

Calling into question the necessity of something like sex education as it currently exists is often met skeptically, if not with laughter and disdain, particularly because of what I read as a deep faith in policy-oriented movements toward justice. This faith has resulted in decades of research and advocacy for policies that police the boundaries of inclusion and exclusion. However, these practices neglect at least two underlying epistemological issues. First, when it comes to adjudicating and organizing human life and its value, the turn toward policy always enacts what Sara Ahmed terms "straightening."[3] That is, policies only ever *differently* organize difference, but also through the *same* commitment to Western Enlightenment rationality itself. Imagining new ideals and new objections that demand adherence to such values in exchange for being seen as a legitimate being only reaffirms the very idea of rationality that I have named as violent throughout this book. Second, the implementation of such a rearrangement is an act that, in and of itself, reifies the logics and epistemological grounds that we must challenge.

Apart from these blind spots, there are at least four other reasons to problematize the turn to policy in attempting to challenge the violence inherent to contemporary sex education. First, policy-oriented change does not in and of itself promise experiential or epistemological change. Changes in policy, or using policy to enact change, can only do so much when it comes to guaranteeing adherence. They enact foreclosures no matter the intention, delineating what should not be done just as much as what should be done and construct narratives around what is "bad" as much as what is "good" without being clear about the underlying normative assumptions. This means that policies tend to perpetuate certain normative frameworks without having to be explicit about whose experiences, voices, and desires are guiding their construction. State-sponsored policy is almost always treated as disembodied in this way, distanced from its creators, the historical context out of which it emerged, and the material conditions to which it refers. Wanda Pillow clearly outlines the way policy, including educational policy, approaches embodiment and offers a valuable critique of "institutionalized policies":

> institutionalized policies often have many shortcomings and may even serve to debilitate the exact condition they wish to advocate. Yet, despite this influx of critique and critical discussion, the arena of policy studies remains dependent upon a technical-rational assessment framework to predict, influence and explain the policy process from development to implementation and outcome, even while those involved in the policy process find it to be highly politicized and even irrational.[4]

Through Pillow's work, we can more readily understand the limited value of reliance upon state policy for addressing the violence of sex education, particularly because it creates a void wherein the voices and embodied experiences of marginalized individuals ought otherwise exist. So, the possibility of advancing any kind of material change through policy is neither ensured nor likely to the extent that state policy works primarily at the level of disembodied, institutionalized norms.

Second, I want to explicitly resist the assumption that education is merely a formalized system of policies and doctrines which grounds the common practice of promoting new policies and doctrines in order to "improve" education. When educational research and scholarship is oriented primarily around policy, it perpetuates, or reinvests in, an understanding of education as a system of policies. The appeal of policy-oriented research is understandable; making policy recommendations grounded in critical research is both important and rewarding, in all senses of the word. It offers a sense of agency that is so often absent in such research, particularly in a political climate that remains generally uninterested in research that does not ultimately affirm the status quo. However, as recent history suggests, it is that policy changes are limited in substantive efficacy. The *why* of this is, I think, latent in the narrow definition of education that policy-oriented research depends upon. Education can and must be understood as a much more diverse set of experiences, physically, mental, and affective, that is always already implicated in and through logics of sexuality, race, class, ability, nationality, and ethnicity.

These *logics* can always resist foreclosure in the face of formalized policy adjustment, even as they make it difficult for so many *people* to do the same. Education remains, in many ways, untouchable, unreachable, inaccessible to state-sponsored policy, as it is always overflowing and meandering beyond what policy can promise. For all that it delineates, there is always excess in both directions due to the natural variety of individuals, locales, social and political contexts, and of economic situations of school districts, schools, classrooms, or classes. If we grant this, then at least some energy ought to be given to this excess, to those moments that policy does not reach, to the experiences that cannot be either dictated or avoided given any particular policy. Policy therefore offers something more akin to an illusion or, to use the language of Stefano Harney and Fred Moten, a trick. They argue that, because policy aims at changes in management, so to speak, it is more aptly described as "resistance from above;" the act of making policy for others, of pronouncing others as incoherent, is at the same time an audition for a post-fordist economy that deputies believe rewards those who embrace change but which, in reality, arrests them in contingency, flexibility, and that administered precarity that imagines itself to be immune from what Judith Butler might call our undercommon precariousness.[5]

Policy reform can cause an almost anesthetizing experience, creating a "willingness to be made contingent and to make contingent all around you. It is a demonstration designed to separate you from others, in the interest of a universality reduced to private property that is not yours, that is the fiction of your own advantage."[6] Resisting the urge to locate the possibility of new worlds—or, refusing to succumb to the allure that is resigning to this world as the pinnacle of progress—is, therefore, essential to any kind of liberatory praxis.

Third, if policy is an attempt to capture, it is worth considering escapist praxes, or to "invent the means in a common experiment launched from any kitchen, any back porch, any basement, any hall, any park bench, any improvised party, every night."[7] I want to be escapist in the face of sex education's inherent violence, and to plan for something different. I am also interested in allowing this project to create a space for exploring the conditions under which different interventions might take place without adhering to the normative structures to which state policy is always committed. By advocating for change that is located more at the experiential level, or that enacts epistemological shifts in experience and the psyche, I am expressing my own desire to participate in something that cultivates alternative subjectivities that themselves might, even momentarily, escape state containment.

This is my final concern with policy-oriented research, then: it is limited to the demands and desires of the state. If, however, it is precisely the state that is using sex education to enact and normalize violence, then reliance on the state must be refused. Or, at the very least, more time, energy, and resources need to be invested into exploring the informal, non-state-run, unhinged practices, experiences, events, and relations that are always at play despite policy's enactment. To be clear, I am not suggesting here that *all* state-sponsored policy is unimportant or ineffective. My contention is that the ways in which they are effective do not always, if ever, align with the stated intentions for which they were conceived, and thus their importance and their effects rarely have the desired results that are assumed to be promised when policies are institutionalized. Further, when entrenched within a state that can only be maintained through violence, this dissonance can be especially dangerous if ignored. All federal sex education policies explored in previous chapters attempt to delineate, through lists and expectations, what is to be taught and for what ends (and of course, how much money is to be allotted for the tasks being addressed). At best, they aim to create conditions under which certain outcomes can both be created and tracked. And we should be careful and attentive to the impossibility of acting outside the state, especially when the relationship between the state and capitalism leaves little room to imagine the former without the latter.[8] However, because of the overwhelming amount of research dedicated to the sliver of the state, real or not, that is potentially nonviolent and/or operating independently of market interests, I want to be stubborn and uncompromised in committing my energy to aim at refusal.

Within sex education policy, these limits are particularly salient as proposed policy-oriented changes are always articulated as requirements for particular kinds of discussions to take place, specific topics to be covered, and certain attitudes toward difference to be encouraged. Within the liberal tradition more specifically, the hope is that students come to feel free and open to new perspectives and undergo an educative experience that allows for comfort and vulnerability, growth, and engagement with others. However, no policy does this, and, even if any did, they can provide no guarantee. We know, for instance, that abstinence-only or -centered programs largely alienate or solidify students' views, both of which can be understood as a kind of violence. Further, politics of inclusion can require violence as well, as in the way that the promise of inclusion always demands some kind of straightening. In this way, policy-oriented changes are often ill-equipped to undermine violence. For this reason, though, continued recognition of the state will *always* be necessary; the cultivation of something beyond the state, if it is possible, requires acknowledgment of it, but it is my hope that the previous chapters support cultivating a practice of attempted refusal.

If there is an alliance that I do have with policy studies, however, it is with those within policy studies who are critical of the relationship between policy and power. For example, Levinson, Sutton, and Winstead argue, "Policy often has the status of a governing text, and this text is variably successful in binding people to its mandates when actually circulated through a social field."[9] In challenging the "normative sense of policy," the authors point to the role of power in determining how policy is created, and by whom it is created, and seek an understanding of policy that aims at democracy as opposed to merely maintaining the power of particular groups.[10] They argue that policy ought to be seen as a practice—or, through a practice approach. They therefore distance themselves from traditional concerns with creating guidelines for enacting policies by situating policy implementation as about "the making of meaning;" policy is instead "always negotiated in social life; values are never fixed but rather contingent on the mobilization of meaning in specific situations."[11] This understanding of policy immediately implicates the community out of which policy is created, as it is only with a shared language, material existence, and culture that policy comes to have cohesive import to any individual goal. While this understanding of policy formation and implementation is far more grounded in community than one merely created by the state, it is unclear how such a policy framework might undermine or disrupt state power when the issue at hand is one that is contingent upon state doctrine, as is the case of sex education. Moving forward, then, I want to revel in the other ways in which education and politics might be harnessed for nonviolent purposes.

Turning Toward Pedagogies

The question of this chapter—what are we to do now?—requires cautious answering, especially because of my reticence to *do* much of anything in the way action and resistance are defined through neoliberal discourses advanced by contemporary comprehensive sex education policies and advocates. The need for caution is bound to the ease with which resistance and reimagining can be violent, too. I am thinking specifically of Reddy's claim about the ways the very concept of knowledge can be defined so as to refuse certain groups' access to the realm of the "knowledgeable;" the incitement must therefore begin with the everyday experiences of those whose ways of knowing and being are excluded from such institutions, though also always implicated by them. Reddy argues,

> To the degree that the norms exist and present themselves as transhistorical, and promise temporal perpetuity, the "other"—the people excluded from the norms—will always be the face of those norms. . . . These norms powerfully shape what we seek to know when addressing the excluded faces of the

norm, and how we apprehend that excluded face, as well as which gives that face its unity and representative coherence for us.[12]

This point is crucial: Reddy challenges us to resist idealizing what we discover in others' epistemological blind spots and shadows because of the blind spots that doing so creates. Instead, *inspiration* for new epistemological frameworks ought to be sought in the blind spots, not *solutions*. And one way of navigating this is by playing with pedagogy.

To summarize, then, this turn toward *sexual pedagogies* is different than proposing an alternative form of sex education in three important ways. First, it *resists* an understanding of education as a formalized system of policies and doctrines that can only be improved through new policies and doctrines. Second, it *refuses* from the get-go the logic that one's sexual education can be adequately addressed in classes and experiences separate and distinct from all other aspects of one's education, as if sexuality is not present in other aspects of education and schooling and as if such classes are sufficient spaces for being sexually educated. Instead, this understanding of pedagogy points to an understanding of education as a diverse set of experiences that is always already implicated in and by logics of sexuality, race, class, economy, and nationality, thus allowing for the creation of alternative educative practices that work to redefine, challenge, resist, and survive such logics in creative, always changing ways. Ultimately, at stake is being able to navigate the water between critique and possibility, or between refusal and demand, or between the present and the future. No matter how the jump is framed, it is only imagination that can make the leap, and therefore the heart of cultivating alternative sexual pedagogies lies in the ability to imagine something different.

Imaginative Impossibilities

When it comes to those ideas most important to my own understanding of how to cultivate these new pedagogies, I am indebted to those working to theorize and practice radical imagination. Radical imagination is necessary for the task of conceiving new, alternative sexual pedagogies insofar as it, as an academic practice and discourse, creates new possibilities for the future by understanding the present differently. There is plenty of scholarly work on imagination in education, but I turn to its radical form, particularly as it emerges out of Queer of Color scholarship, insofar as it is only here that race, class, and sexuality are taken seriously in the *work* of imagining, rather than merely as *subjects* of imagination, as will be discussed later in the chapter. Given that imagination has a rich history in educational theory, I want to distance myself from such traditions by addressing the work of Maxine Greene and Henry Giroux.

For Greene, a lack of imagination in education is evidenced by the "sense of repetitiveness and uniformity" which works to "discourage active learning."[13] Imagination thus plays a constructive role, enabling the possibility of "becoming different," or of "the ability to look at things as if they could be otherwise."[14] Imagination, for Greene, begins with an openness to these possibilities and is followed by an action based upon them: only by being open to different futures and to imagining that things could be different does the work of imagination take place. Further, imagination is important, according to Greene, at all levels of education, and for anyone from parents to administrators to students to teachers. What imagination does, she argues, is enable empathy between and for difference, resist processes of normalization, and help to "decenter" participants in ways that are necessary for breaking such normative processes.[15] She relies heavily on art and aesthetics as spaces for imagination and risk, because it is in art, she argues, that one can experience each of these aspects of imagination and produce new social visions. Greene grounds knowledge production in the conscious questioning of what others offer us as reality and in the naming of obstacles or problems that perpetuate student oppression or limit the possibility of freedom.

It is imagination, on Greene's account, that is crucial to this initial step of becoming conscious, and then to being able to name the obstacles to one's freedom. She says, "To tap into imagination is to become able to break with what is supposedly fixed and finished, objectively, independently real. It is to see beyond what the imaginer has called normal or 'common sensical' and to carve our new orders in experience."[16] Though imagination as a way of thinking is essential in general to breaking with the status quo, which is assumed to be oppressive, it is specifically imagining that things could be other than they are that opens up what she calls a "space of freedom" in which one can exercise agency as a free human.[17] In this way, imagination is a privileged form of knowledge creation and way of knowing because of its potential to create new understandings of the world, new knowledge of one's situation, and new solutions to the obstacles one faces to their liberation. I do not think that

Greene is wrong about the possibilities inherent to teaching through and for imagination in general in education; however, it is striking that her analysis only addresses oppression vaguely, as an object for imagination. Nowhere does Greene explore or analyze the way oppression and violence can interact with imagination, and how imagination might relate to the material world differently for different people.

Giroux's work delves deeper into imagination's limits in education, primarily because he situates his analysis of the relationship between education and imagination within the context of neoliberalism. Neoliberalism, he argues, is a logic based on the marriage of capitalism to liberal values such that freedom, value, and equality are determined largely through market value. In education, these logics reduce students to "consuming and marketable subjects." Further, he notes that an effect of this reduction is the relegation of students who deviate from the norms asserted by that logic to marginal and exploitable positions. Neoliberalism also represents the replacement of creativity, imagination, and, in many ways, education itself, with market-driven reform, standardization, instrumental rationality, and the "pursuit of profits." Challenging neoliberalism is thus best done through pedagogies that posit a view of the student as an active co-investigative agent capable of participating in the naming of their reality and as capable of imagining different futures. Again, it is not the case that I disagree with this perspective; however, it remains insufficient to the task of addressing the violence I have described. We need more than a rethinking of our view of the student, or even ourselves. Instead, we need a radical rethinking of the structure of our society and education's place within it. This is what the work of radical imagination does.[18]

Located within discourses around both Black studies' and Queer of Color studies' efforts to engage in futuristic thinking, radical imaginative endeavors shamelessly catapult us into the impossible while still maintaining an intimate relationship to the here and now, especially the political here and now. Robin G. D. Kelley's work is especially inspiring on these points.

For Kelley, radical imagination is inherently creative, poetic, and powerful and is aimed specifically at new understandings of identity. Speaking of the kind of imagination his mother cultivated within him, Kelley says,

> She simply wanted us to live through our third eyes, to see life as possibility. She wanted us to imagine a world free of patriarchy, a world where gender

and sexual relations could be reconstructed. She wanted us to see the poetic and prophetic in the richness of our daily lives. She wanted us to visualize a more expansive, fluid, "cosmos-politan" definition of blackness, to teach us that we are not merely inheritors of a culture but its makers.[19]

The role of radical imagination is to bring to fruition a relationship between oneself and a different future, to disrupt one's imaginary attachments to the realities of everyday life, and instead locate them in a future "nowhere," a place that is not here, but a place that exists solely in the imagination.[20] This means that, on Kelley's account, radical imagination does not envision what is possible but creates new worlds that motivate political action: "My point is that the *dream of a new world*, my mother's dream, was the catalyst for my own political engagements."[21] A resistance to imagination that is limited by the present, combined with an understanding of the impossible novelty as an instigator of political action, makes radical imagination itself inherently political.

This understanding of imagining new worlds, which then orient and motivate political action, also takes seriously the affective or felt aspect of such work. This aspect of radical imagination is where one's experiences in the world come into play most powerfully—the affective experience of imagining radically is deeply rooted in one's experiences with race, gender, class, and sexuality. This brings to mind Phillip Brian Harper's argument about "felt intuition": or "evidence of things not seen."[22] For Harper, felt intuition is the answer to an essential, ever-confounding question: "How [do we] consider the meaning of an experience no concrete evidence of which exists, and of which we can therefore claim no positive knowledge?"[23] The possibility of disrupting the current epistemological order requires beginning with a view of experience that itself is scorned by such an order, and this is what the affective can offer.[24]

At stake in the centering of the affective are new "nowheres." Kelley turns to both love and surrealism, particularly as they emerge from and exist in Afrodiasporic culture, to articulate this. Love and surrealism are crucial to the task of radical imagination insofar as they explicitly act against calls for practicality and rationality, and against dominant systems of power and state violence, thus marking them as central to the actual, tangible, felt work of making "nowheres" possible. The entire purpose of surrealism, in fact, is transformation: "[The surrealists] are speaking of new social relationships, new ways of living and interacting, new attitudes towards work and leisure and community."[25] A surrealist- and love-inspired understanding of imagination is thus perfectly situated for the task of dismantling the violence within federal sex education by creating an environment within which radical imagination might bloom.

There is a sense of utopianism at play here that deserves attention. Kelley's work is explicitly utopian in nature insofar as it understands the relationship between imagination and political change as located in the possibility of imagining new futures. The creation of different worlds depends first on being able to imagine them. As Kelley argues,

> Progressive social movements do not simply produce statistics and narratives of oppression; rather, the best ones do what great poetry always does: transport us to another place, compel us to relive horrors and, more importantly, enable us to imagine a new society. We must remember that the conditions and the very existence of social movements enable participants to imagine something different, to realize that things need not always be this way. It is *that* imagination, that effort to see the future in the present, that I shall call "poetry" or "poetic knowledge."[26]

As such, radical imagination inaugurates utopian considerations insofar as it requires the creation of different pasts and new futures that we can imaginatively and affectively move ourselves from and into, just as a poem does. It also posits an intimate relationship between the past, present, and future and enacts affective and real changes that spark the need for something different. For Kelley, it is hope that is at stake, and that hope is a collective one. In the following excerpt from his reading of Grace Lee Boggs, Kelley offers a clear description of what the process of utopian imagination might look like:

> What we need to do . . . is encourage groups of all kinds and all ages to participate in creating a vision of the future that will enlarge the humanity of all of us and then, in devising concrete programs on which they can work together, if only in a small way, to move toward their vision. In this unique interim time between historical epochs, this is how we can elicit the hope that is essential to the building of a movement and unleash the energies that in the absence of hope are turned against other people or even against oneself. . . . When people come together voluntarily to create their own vision, they begin wishing it to come into being with such passion that they begin creating an active path leading to it from the present. The spirit and the way to make the spirit live coalesce.[27]

It is this view of utopia, I am arguing, that ought to ground our reimagining of education, and of its relationship to sexuality, in the task of conceiving of nonviolent sexual pedagogies in public schools.

That being said, the specific kind of evocation of utopian thought that I am most compelled by is motivated by Kathi Week's understanding of utopian demands, an understanding that I believe aligns well with Kelley's own utopian interests by virtue of their shared use of the idea of hope. Weeks sets out to develop, based significantly on the work of Ernst Bloch and Friedrich Nietzsche, an alternative vision of utopia and hope, more immune to liberal critiques of utopianism as naive. Her aim is to "explore hope as a mode of temporality, a cognitive and affective relation to time and a way to approach the relationships among historicity, presentism and futurity."[28] For Weeks, following the work of Bloch, hope is "a cognitive faculty and an emotion" and must be so in order to prompt utopian thinking that is itself both oriented toward *both* the possible and the impossible, the real and the beyond, the "new that is familiar."[29] However, this means hoping for what we do not know. Acknowledging this, Weeks argues that if "wanting a different future and making it may not hinge on knowing what it might be," then the affective dimension of hope can act as a political and epistemological force, fueling participation in the project of hope and also the envisioning of the radically different and other future.[30] This affective dimension of hope, though, is somewhat paradoxical, because it ultimately asks the subject to "create some distance between the present and the sometimes crushing determinative power of the past in order to be strong enough to will a new future, in which the self we affirm would no longer exist."[31] The idea of "willing to become otherwise" is thus central to this affective dimension of hope; one must want or desire that which does not exist so that one remains open to the possibility that such a future does not include the self that exists now. Loving and perishing, creation and destruction, guide hope's affective task.[32] In tune with each other here, both Kelley and Weeks understand that affirming the role of affect in conceptions of utopia strikes a nerve for some attempting to rationalize utopian possibilities by challenging the assumption that the only *useful* or *rational* view of the future is one that can be analytically described and mapped. Instead, when rooted in epistemological assumptions about the centrality of affect to understanding and knowledge creation, the experiences of contradiction, paradox, and indetermination can be invaluable in the work of *envisioning*, not *knowing*, what is to come.

The idea of utopian demands, then, emerges as Weeks's way to "stimulate the imagination of what might become rather than nostalgia for what once was; and also mobilize on the basis of hope for a different future, rather than only an outrage and resentment over past and present injustices."[33] This kind of hope itself provokes that Weeks calls "breaks," which do just that: they split off from what we are supposed to cling to. These ideas affirm the concerns with policy-oriented change under interrogation here, as utopian demands project desires that are incapable of being contained by "policy proposals" because they do not need to rationally explain the aims of the break they intend from the present.[34] It is the provocation that such demands create, *not* the mere implementation of what has been otherwise articulated as the "way forward." If no policy or reform can ever fully encompass the power and potentiality of the utopian demand, then those invested in the role of education in inciting breaks need not confine themselves to the administrative or curricular demands of our current age of reformism. Instead, we might look to the ways in which we can engage with our students' subjectivity, regardless of, or perhaps even within, current or future policy plans. In this way, a turn toward pedagogies coincides with utopian demands in the move to understand and focus on the everyday educative experiences. If the task is to conceive of nonviolent pedagogies in public schools, then utopian demands become an important source for cultivating the imagination needed to do so.

Hope, not Happiness, not Humanization

The centrality of hope within the kind of utopian demands that I am advocating for here begs an important question, specifically important given its relationship to education, about the *kind* of hope that might foster such demands: Might hope bring us happiness? Education in general, and schooling in particular, so often posits happiness as the intended goal of the experiences it provides that speaking of hope in relation to education makes it particularly susceptible to a kind of optimism that I want to explicitly reject. There is an important difference between the kind of hope that drives radical utopian imagining and demanding and the kind of hope that constitutes the cruel optimism discussed earlier.

In a discussion for *Women & Performance*, Lisa Duggan shares with José Esteban Muñoz that she is "interested" in the idea shared by a friend that "Hope is the worst thing."[35] Reflecting on this, she writes that "When I think about *hope*, I set it alongside *happiness* and *optimism*, which I immediately associate with race and class privilege, with imperial hubris, with gender and sexual conventions, with maldistributed forms of security both national personal," which leads her to ask: "Can collective hope without delusion or guarantees generate future possibilities beyond any present expectation? Can those of us without happiness or optimism (however otherwise ecstatic we might nonetheless be) generate collective hope now? Or can such hope be a sop, a con, a misdirection of collective energies?"[36] These questions are echoed in what Sara Ahmed writes about "the promise of happiness," or a "conditional happiness," a shared object of desire that allows us to "get along" so long as we are "willing and able to express happiness in proximity to the right things."[37] Though each does so differently, both Duggan and Ahmed express a concern for the ways that happiness—and the hopes or promises it carries—enact the very violence that I am arguing sex education makes possible.

Muñoz, sympathetic to the concern, offers a remedy that is similarly valuable in light of this interpretation of sex education: educated hope. Careful to resist creating a "strangling binary between good hope and bad hope," he argues that educated hope is one that "helps escape from a script in which human existence is reduced."[38] In *Cruising Utopia*, we find a more elaborate explanation of the reasons such a hope matters. Here, Muñoz famously argues that "queerness is not yet here"; instead, it is a "longing that propels us onward, beyond the romances of the negative and toiling in the present. Queerness is that thing that lets us feel that this world is not enough, that indeed something is missing." The point is, in part, that educated hope is inherently queer because of its political orientation away from the scripts provided by a society structured through violent logics. Educated hope is not a bad-feeling hope, they both argue, as it is better understood in opposition to complacency, or to a riskless acceptance of the "constraints of the present conditions."[39]

Of large concern throughout this project is how sex education attempts to enact a kind of subjectification oriented toward the legitimization of violence has been and remains attached to the idea of the human and the process of humanization. Educated hope, however, also offers a way to crack these attachments and enables the utopian demands I am arguing ought to be considered as pedagogical necessities for those who desire even a less-violent future. This idea of educated hope offered in Muñoz's work therefore helps get us out of some of this humanism.[40] He writes,

> To think the inhuman is the necessary queer labor of the incommensurate. The fact that this thing we call the inhuman is never fully knowable, because of our own stuckness within humanity, makes it a kind of knowing that is incommensurable with the protocols of human knowledge production. Despite the incommensurability, this seeming impossibility, one must persist in thinking in these inhuman directions.[41]

Queerness, according to Muñoz, and in line with other Queer of Color critiques, including Ahmed's, is a necessary component of antiviolent utopian thought insofar as it can be used to dismantle normative constructions of gender, race, sexuality, and class, and also insofar as it can push us to imagine nonhuman or inhuman ways of being that transgress each of these categories and thus betray the idea of the human itself. This is why educated hope is also a *critical hope*: it resides in ways of knowing and meaning-making that negate the assumption of Western rationalism that all opposition is acknowledgment and thus impossible. Muñoz therefore helps guide the imagining of alternative sexual pedagogies by offering a view of queer, educated, critical utopian hope that is especially prepared to motivate the construction of utopian demands that might actually destabilize education's relationship to violence.

Stuplimity, Pessimism, and Clandestine Pedagogies

Though I find much that is desirable in Muñoz's educated hope, I want to briefly offer a version of critical hope that is more associated with negative emotions. The danger of aligning hope with normative subjunctivization is always lurking nearby, and the work of clarifying a hope that is unlikely to slide into something akin to Berlant's cruel optimism, or what Terry Eagleton calls the lapse of "hope into self-delusion," is never inherently effective; it is *no* promise. This danger is always haunting hope, threatening to impede the process of imagining alternatives and desiring new futures. Grounding hope in queerness does not itself protect against this, either. I think this is especially true in educative spaces, wherein the restraints placed on queerness and the orientation towards happiness or other overly "positive" emotions are so endemic and undermine the political possibilities lying in wait in radical hope. Meeting such positivity with "inappropriate" affect is thus a compelling possible response. More accurately, exploring the experiences and arguments of those who respond to positivity in a way that is likely to be perceived by others as "strange" or "wrong" or "abnormal," not merely "negative," offers an inciting and exciting glimmer of novelty.

Following Sianne Ngai's account of what she calls "ugly feelings," the significance of locating political potential in responses to the world that are incongruent with the norm is helpful in refusing the deeply normative notion of happiness in education. In discussing the *"critical* productivity" of these "dysphoric affects," Ngai details how transnational capitalism, with its trend toward affective homogenization around race and sexuality, produces excess and failure, both spaces within which lie lessons about politics.[42] The harder it gets to see, hear, and sense these failures, though, the more important they become: "The evidence here would suggest that the very effort of thinking the aesthetic and political together—a task whose urgency seems to increase in proportion to its difficulty in a [sic] increasingly anti-utopian and functionally differentiated society—is a prime occasion for ugly feelings."[43] Case in point: stuplimity.

Stuplimity references an affective response comprised of two seemingly "antithetical" experiences: shock and boredom.[44] Indeed, envisioned in relation to aesthetics, and derived from Ngai's work within literary theory, the concept of stuplimity is always political and thus, considering it alongside education's demand for happiness despite its crumbling existence, is provocative of what might appear in the midst of this crumbling. There is, Ngai notes, a relation to the sublime here, though not just as a shared experience of terror, awe, and/or serenity (following Kant); the sublimity conjured in this aesthetic experience can also evoke an *"inability* of other mental activities, including reason, to overcome an affective state."[45] In moments of shock and astonishment, then, experiences of exhaustion, fatigue, and even boredom, or *stuplimity,* can exist, too.

Stuplimity refers, then, to a resistance to romancitizations of the sublime, a resistance that is derived from the fatigue sublime can induce by virtue of its overwhelming and often incomprehensible nature.[46] The "dysphoria of shock and boredom," however, creates what Ngai describes as

> an "open feeling" of "resisting being"—an indeterminate affective state that lacks the punctuating "point" of an individuated emotion. In other words, the negative affect of stuplimity might be said to produce another affective state in its wake, a secondary feeling that seems strangely neutral, unqualifies, "open." . . . Yet in generating a form of "open feeling" in its wake, stuplimity leaves us precisely in a place to [imagine].[47]

And, because of this openness, the almost free for all that is made possible by such fatigue and boredom, "this final outcome of stuplimity—the echo or afterimage produced by it, as it were—makes possible a kind of resistance."[48] Stuplimity can open moments of possibility and difference. I want to be careful here: nowhere does Ngai suggest that these moments are signals of "solutions" or secret portholes to new worlds. Her final words on stuplimity are, instead, telling of the breaks it can cause, not its resolutions. She writes of "going limp or falling down" as affective ugliness that requires different attention and praxes than what we are typically prepared for.[49] That is, in the face of the demand to succumb to the promise of a beautiful and happy future that is offered by sex education, Ngai's stuplimity points to ruptures and refusals that are likely to seem absurd, nauseating, harmful, and even insane.[50] But, if we take this work seriously, if we leave open for even a moment the possibility that something different lies in, to call upon Christina Sharpe's imagery, "the wake,"[51] what else might emerge?

Alas, who am I to say? I, myself, remain embedded in many of the very systems that keep us distant from something different. Academic critique itself, such as what I've laid out here, is overwhelmingly limited by the demand for the kind of rationalization that I have described as violent. As Stefano Harney and Fred Moten argue in *The Undercommons*, even when housed in academia (perhaps even *especially* when housed here), and even when touted by "critical" scholars, critique "endangers the sociality it is supposed to defend."[52] Again, to be clear and careful, my own position in the academy, among other positions that I occupy related to my identity and material experience, undermines my own ability to move beyond critique, in the sense that Harney and Moten point to as necessary, and I have no intention of pretending this is not the case. But, in invoking this work, this destruction of what I have been sold and have bought into as the horizon of critical, radical, academic politics, perhaps a crack is made somewhere, somehow. Again, Harney and Moten remind us, "it's evil and uncool to have a place in the sun in the dirty thinness of this atmosphere; . . . the house the sheriff was building is in the heart of a fallout zone."[53] Our reliance, however critical, on sex education policy reform to address systematic violence, in and beyond schooling, is merely a commitment to the illusion of safety, comfort, and progress, and to the luxury promised, that holds up this house and I hope only to do what I can to participate in the cracking of its foundation.

To this end, the ideas of radical imagination, utopian demands, queer critical hope, and a kind of apathetic-to-your-expectations pessimism inspire within me something like a demand for clandestine pedagogies. At least, that is what I desire in my head, in my body, in my experience in the world as a result of the free, spontaneous interplay I have tried to allow them in my engagement with them over the years. I will, of course, change, and so will my relationship to these ideas, and, in the process, my understanding of the quality and content of clandestine pedagogies will also change. And, as promised, I will *not* tell you what to do with this idea. I will not tell you how to define it. I will not tell you what it looks like. I will not tell you anything more than what I already have. Instead, in what follows, I offer potentially motivating ideas, each one suggestive of what might become, somehow, a utopian demand for those driven by a desire, in whatever ways, to bring about different relations between education and sexuality and to do so with a similar pedagogical desire: to become clandestine.

Conclusion

Clandestine Praxes

In 1993, Octavia Butler's *Parable of the Sower* was first published. The novel is the first in a series of speculative fiction that follows a fifteen-year-old Black girl named Lauren as she embarks upon a journey that is both oriented away from and toward: away from devastation and toward the uncertain. The devastation reads as possible to me: social, political, and economic ruins that result from increasing economic inequity and the destruction of the climate. The uncertain reads as less so, but in part because what was once far away is now near—the book is set in 2025, now only four years away from the moment in which I write—but it is also a future that unravels as Lauren moves about herself. Butler builds a world in which, when faced with death, of the self and of those with whom Lauren has formed all kinds of intimate relations, Lauren also faces possibility. She wanders away from her family, her friends, her lover, her home, with only a knapsack, seeking little but survival. The "little" is important, though: it is a hint, a feeling, of a new form of understanding that is borne out of Lauren's uniquely empathetic wiring, or hyperempathy (she feels for herself the actual pain and pleasures experienced by others along with them), and her emergent beliefs about the nature of existence. Experienced together, Lauren imagines Earthseed, the name she gives to her set of beliefs. Earthseed is presented less as universal than as always in the process of becoming and holds fast to this core expression:

> All that you touch
> You change.

> All that you Change
> Changes you.

> The only lasting truth
> is Change.

God

Is Change.

As Lauren moves further and further away from her past life, she experiences all kinds of change, interacts with all kinds of agents, and is changed, herself, along the way. She forms relations of all kinds, too, many of which amount to forms of intimacy that are currently impossible, at least within a world tethered to its white, capitalist, and settler heteronormative assumptions about truth and goodness. A young, full, complicated Black girl offers us a glimpse at a future that is beautifully different.

Just over twenty years later, in 2015, Nnedi Okorafor's *Binti* was published. *Binti*, the first in a speculative trilogy, follows its protagonist, a young, female Himba (a human group inspired by the real Himba tribe that is indigenous to what is now Northern Namibia) girl named Binti, who also comes to us from the future. For Binti, the journey to be taken is one across space and time and less for the sake of physical survival than a sort of psychic survival: an educational one. Binti, after taking a series of planetary exams in Mathematics, has been identified as highly intelligent and immediately admitted into Oomza University, a university elsewhere in the galaxy. Further, if she accepts the admittance, she will be the first Himba human to attend. However, she says that "No matter what choice I made, I was never going to have a normal life, really."[1] The lack of a so-called choice is a result of her own unique differences, and not just as the first Himba human to embark on this journey. She is, we learn, a "harmonizer," who is described as having the ability to communicate with bodies and spirit flows in unprecedented ways.[2] She is already so different from others, and yet it is this difference that leads her to accept more uncertainty, more unfamiliarity. She decides to go because "I wanted . . . I needed it."[3] Binti makes the leap, leaves without saying goodbye to her family ("Death. When I left my home, I died."[4]), and boards the ship "Third Fish," an amphibious technological life-form that acts as a form of intergalactic transportation. As she moves further from home, she, too, learns more about herself than she ever could have otherwise imagined, forms relationships—across species—that she never knew were possible, and learns to enact community across differences in ways that certainly seem impossible now. Again, a young, full, complicated African girl offers us a glimpse at a future that is beautifully different.

Parable and *Binti* do *not* offer the same story; it is clear from the first words that each author tells an exceptionally unique story about incredibly distinct girls and build dazzlingly different worlds in the process. But what they share, the iterations of possibility that they enact when put alongside each other, are nonetheless powerful in their own respects. They both are different *because* they have a mostly clandestine, not fully understood capacity to connect with others. These capacities are not ones that appeal to contemporary neoliberal conceptions of ability, either; in fact, they are arguably capabilities that purposefully destabilize the concept of the ability itself. Further, these differences make them suspicious and even dangerous to some as they continue their journeys. They are threats to and therefore threatened by those who do not understand them, or who see no value in their lives other than as material to be consumed in various ways. They both witness murder, and experience starvation and alienation, too. But in the process, they also learn more about themselves and discover the depths of their own capabilities around communication, coalition, and communion. They are full of impossible possibilities that have import for them but not *just* them. They travel away from the most likely future and into a new, seemingly unlikely, further future, where new ways of being and learning and loving come into fruition.

Both of these stories, both of these Afro-futuristic dreams, hold so much possibility, and it matters that the possibilities are ultimately left undefined by the end of their respective journeys. Both characters experience desirous sparks given their own situatedness and senses of self that expose cracks within the given and make possible an impossible future that, among many other things, exposes its readers to cracks in their worlds, too. They certainly did—and continue to, every time I engage or teach with them—for me. They enact a tension, too, between the desire to hope for changes to what is and the desire for something that is not currently here. There are drastic steps to be taken. The costs are high. But they are never higher than the cost of staying still. Caught between choices that are not really choices—to live or to die; to stay or to grow—Lauren and Binti offer a different option. Borne of the belief in the magic of the excess, they point those willing to notice toward the refusal of the choice itself. They point to something beyond mere survival, beyond mere change, beyond mere settling. They choose what is otherwise depicted itself as impossible: to grow, to create, to live out and as something different. Of course, when I read and reread these stories, I know that I cannot, by virtue of my own existence as a white woman, lay claim to much, and I even know that they might not be for or about me. But they still make me feel both fired up and ferocious, and maybe that is an additional sign of their power: to do that for those who desire something else. They show what it might look like to refuse in a way that is life-opening and -expanding. As I reflect on the ways I benefit from what they know is life-closing, I also recognize that they make it possible to imagine a world in which saying what I will now say is the most realistic, possible, rigorous, caring, concrete thing to say: *This is not the world for me.*

So, to the limits placed on theorizing by the present state of sex education, including those who work rigorously to reform and revitalize the role of sexuality education in schools, I therefore say, "not this."[5] Confronted by an overwhelming failure to address the violence smuggled into education, and public schools in the United States, through federally funded sex education for over 100 years, by virtue of its refusal to do anything other than delineate human life through the promotion of exclusionary and marginalizing conceptions of knowledge and rationality, I shall, following Sara Ahmed, offer a swift, disinterested eye roll and instead, allow myself to be distracted by what is aligned with my desires for something different, knowing that this desire is always only possible for me because of the impossible things that have been done by these nonwhite, deviant, out-of-this-world girls.

There is so much to learn from those who distract us from the confines of what is possible. Left to linger, these desires, these ways of being, in their full, complicated existence, can alter our educational habits and might even provoke glimpses into what I am calling the clandestine: secretive, often illicit, covert, hidden, subversive, deceptive, surreptitious, quotidian practices, epistemologies, communing, and laboring that causes cracks and breaks. They overlap and are interdependent and mutually constructed and sometimes contradictory to each other. They also far exceed the glimpses offered here. They are the excess that federally funded education cannot contain and therefore ignores. But their lessons are lying in wait. The very least I can do is acknowledge their beauty, betray what is now itself ugly, and surrender to the educational experiences they offer. Who are the "they"? Them:

The criminal: *"Hustling is a tool of survival for the dispossessed. Yet in putting their sexualities to work, [Black women sex workers] may have seen this tactic as open to revision, mediation, and other worlds of imagination."*[6]

—Mireille Miller-Young

The dependent: *"But a struggle to survive cannot lead to suicide: Suicide is the opposite of survival. And so we must not conceal/assimilate/integrate into the would-be dominant culture and political system that despises us. Our survival requires that we alter our environment so that we can live and so that we can hold each other's hands and so that we can kiss each other on the streets, and in the daylight of our existence, without terror and without violent and sometimes fatal reactions from the busybodies of America."*[7]

—June Jordan

The sentimental: *"I have to remember that no one knew that things would get better, and that even people who were working to make it happen had to live with oppression every day. I read your writing and the writing of your other comrades from that time and I feel grateful. It seems like maybe you knew about us. It feels like you loved us already."*[8]

—Alexis Pauline Gumbs

The fugitive: *"We are the general antagonism to politics looming outside every attempt to politicize, every imposition of self-governance, every sovereign decision and its degraded miniature, every emergent state and home sweet home. We are disruption and consent to disruption. We preserve upheaval. Sent to fulfill by abolishing, to renew by unsettling, to open the enclosure whose immeasurable venality is inversely proportionate to its actual area, we got politics surrounded. We cannot represent ourselves. We can't be represented."*[9]

—Stefano Harney and Fred Moten

The dreamer: *"Trans women are free to live in their skin and not feel like they have to deal with transmisogyny. Life would be so simple. People wouldn't have to worry about moving or missing a meal or if they're going to have to do this or that. We will have everything that we need. Everyone will love each other and we will smoke lots of weed."*[10]

—CeCe McDonald

The demon: "... the demonic invites a slightly different conceptual pathway—while retaining its supernatural etymology—and acts to identify a system (social, geographic, technological) that can only unfold and produce an outcome if uncertainty, or (dis)organization, or something supernaturally demonic, is integral to the methodology."[11]

—Katherine McKittrick

The whore: "Girls, girls, get that cash/If it's 9 to 5 or shaking your ass/Ain't no shame, ladies do your thing/Just make sure you ahead of the game/Just 'cause I got a lot of fame super/Prince couldn't get me change my name, papa/Kunta Kinte a slave again, no sir/Picture blacks saying, 'Oh yes'a, massa' (No!)/Picture Lil' Kim dating a pastor."[12]

—Missy Elliot

The naive: "She asks me questions. Or ... she comes to me, 'Mom, my little friend told me her mom was undocumented too. That's so cool! We both get to spend vacation together [since we can't travel]!' She's so positive."[13]

—Janet Gonzolez, discussing her children with Laura E. Enriquez

The unrealistic: "All organizing is science fiction."[14]

—Whalidah Imarisha

The confusing: "The only thing that makes life possible is permanent, intolerable uncertainty: not knowing what comes next."

—Ursula Le Guin[15]

The inhuman: "This alternative movement, a transvaluation of the human, will require a change in the underlying structures of Man's being/knowing/eeling 'human' in a manner such that we no longer make any reference to the transcendentalist conception that many are eager to move beyond."[16]

—Zakiyyah Iman Jackson

The profane: "[funky erotixxx is] an acknowledgement that what is profane or obscene has a lineage that exceeds its destructive imperialist mandates within Western patriarchy, and that is sacred."[17]

—L. H. Stallings

The irrational: "In the face of these conditions one can only sneak into the university and steal what one can. To abuse its hospitality, to spite its mission, to join its refugee colony, its gypsy encampment, to be in but not of—this is the path of the subversive intellectual in the modern university."[18]

—Stefano Harney and Fred Moten

The sick: "Because a sex life depends upon ability, any departure from sexual norms reads as disability, disease, or defect. . . . What sea change in current scientific, medical, political, and romantic attitudes would be necessary to represent disabled sexuality as a positive contribution to the future."[19]

—Tobin Siebers

The immature: "I'm trying to just serve sexy and confident, whore. Slutty[20] cougar on the prowl. 3rd rate Faith Hill impersonator. 80% sexy, 20% disgusting."[21]

—Katya Zamolodchikova

These glimpses, offered generously by others, point to different educative moments and experiences that, somehow, slowly, might create what I imagine to be a kind of bubble, a space in which our own relationships and understandings and feelings with and of sexuality might be deepened in accordance with their general pursuit of an education that honors any latent desire for something else, however unintelligent, irrational, uneducated, crazy, unrealistic, impossible creating such a bubble might be. Then, I hope that someday this bubble pops, and whatever happens is something that is, well, inconceivable.

Notes

Introduction

1 Prince A. Morrow, "Prophylaxis of Social Diseases," *American Journal of Sociology* 13, no. 1 (July 1907): 21.
2 Ibid., 23.
3 Ibid., 21.
4 Ibid., 28.
5 Ibid., 30.
6 Alexandra Lord, *Condom Nation* (Baltimore: The Johns Hopkins University Press, 2010), 18.
7 Raymond B. Fosdick, "The Commission on Training Camp Activities," *Proceedings of the Academy of Political Science in the City of New York* 7, no. 4 (February 1918), *Social Sciences Index Retrospective: 1929-1983 (H.W. Wilson)*, EBSCOhost (accessed April 10, 2014), 819.
8 Ibid., 825.
9 Ibid., 826.
10 US Public Health Service Treasure Department, "Healthy Happy Womanhood: A Pamphlet for Girls and Young Women" (Washington: Government Printing Office, 1920), 4.
11 Ibid., 5.
12 Ibid., 9–10.
13 Ibid., 10.
14 Ibid., 11.
15 Ibid., 13.
16 Ibid., 16.
17 Before I go any further, I want to clarify that I have almost exclusively considered female or female-identifying sex workers in this project. This is an inherent limitation to this research for two reasons: it assumes that sex is a binary category, which it is not, and it erases sex workers of other genders

and gender expressions from this conversation, which I do not take lightly. I have focused on "women" here because of their dominance in the literature around the problems I explore and because of the targeting of female sexuality and women's bodies that is at the heart of sex education, but I do very much hope that this research applies in some way to the experiences of sex workers across all genders, sexes, and sexualities, and believe that the *implications* of this research do apply broadly.

18 Michel Foucault, "Nietzsche, Genealogy, History," in *Language, Counter-Memory, Practice: Selected Essays and Interviews*, ed. by D. F. Bouchard (Ithaca: Cornell University Press, 1977), 140.

19 Colin Koopman, *Genealogy as Critique: Foucault and the Problems of Modernity* (Bloomington: Indiana University Press, 2013), 4.

20 Foucault, "Nietzsche, Genealogy, History," 142.

21 I will use the word "prostitute" when referring to the discourses that justified the creation of sex education, but I will use the term "sex worker" to refer to anything outside of that, including my own analysis and argumentation. The term "sex worker" is more accurate in capturing the labor and purpose of this kind of work, and it is also used to legitimize the importance and value of those workers as beings whose lives matter, then and now.

22 Lord, *Condom Nation*, 7.

23 Ibid., 28.

24 Valarie Huber and Michal Firmin, "A History of Sex Education in the United States Since 1900," *International Journal of Educational Reform* 23, no. 1 (2014): 27.

25 Lord, *Condom Nation*, 13.

26 Ibid., 19.

27 Jeffrey Moran, *Teaching Sex: The Shaping of Adolescence in the 20th Century* (Cambridge, MA: Harvard University Press, 2000), 28.

28 Ibid., 34.

29 Lord, *Condom Nation*, 17.

30 Ibid., 29.

31 Courtney Q. Shah, *Sex Ed, Segregated: The Quest for Sexual Knowledge in Progressive-Era America* (Rochester: University of Rochester Press, 2015), xiii.

32 Lord, *Condom Nation*, 31.

33 Julian B. Carter, "Birds, Bees, and Venereal Disease: Toward an Intellectual History of Sex Education," *Journal of the History of Sexuality* 2, no. 2 (2001): 241.

34 See Robin Jensen, *Dirty Words: The Rhetoric of Public Sex Education, 1870-1924* (Champaign: University of Illinois Press, 2010).

35 Michel Foucault, *Ethics: Subjectivity and Truth*, ed. by Paul Rabinow, trans. by Robert Hurley and others (New York: W.W. Norton & Co., Inc., 1994), 77.
36 Michel Foucault, "Governmentality," in *The Foucault Effect: Studies in Governmentality*, ed. by Graham Burchell, Colin Gordon and Peter Miller (Chicago: The University of Chicago Press, 1991), 79.
37 Foucault, "Sex, Power and the Politics of Identity," in *Essential Works of Foucault 1954-1984*, ed. by Paul Rabinow (Harmondsworth: Penguin Books, 2000).
38 L. H. Stallings, *Funk the Erotic* (Urbana, Chicago, and Springfield: University of Illinois Press, 2015), 8.
39 Ibid. This understanding of art as experience is inspired partly by John Dewey's work on the topic.
40 I had intended on allowing these comments to exist independently and without my own contextualization as a way to, as mentioned in the Introduction, inspire different thinking in education about sex work through the words of sex workers themselves. For copyright purposes, I have had to incorporate them into the body of the text. I ask the reader to therefore ignore as much of my own words in these short introductory and concluding paragraphs that bookend each chapter and to make your own connections between them and the content of the chapters.
41 Cathy Cohen, "Deviance and Resistance," *Du Bois Review: Social Science Research on Race* 1, no. 1 (2004): 30.

Chapter 1

1 Josephine Baker as detailed in *Josephine: The Hungry Heart* by Jean-Claude Baker, cited in Hadley Hall Meares, "Paris When It Sizzles: The Loves and Lives of Josephine Baker," *Vanity Fair*, September 2, 2020, https://www.vanityfair.com/hollywood/2020/09/josephine-baker-biography-paris.
2 Ibid.
3 Michel Foucault, "The Subject and Power," *Critical Inquiry* 8, no. 4 (Summer 1982): 778.
4 Cathy Cohen, "Punks, Bulldagers, and Welfare Queens: The Radical Potential of Queer Politics?," *GLQ: A Journal of Lesbian and Gay Studies* 3 (1997): 442.
5 Roderick Ferguson, *Aberrations in Black: Toward A Queer of Color Critique* (Minneapolis: University of Minnesota Press, 2003), 3.
6 Ibid., 448.

7. Kyla Wazana Tompkins, "Intersections of Race, Gender, and Sexuality: Queer of Color Critique," in *The Cambridge Companion to American Gay and Lesbian Literature*, ed. by S. Herring (Cambridge: Cambridge University Press, 2015), 173–4.
8. Ibid., 174.
9. Ed Brockenbrough, "Introduction to the Special Issue: Queers of Color and Anti-Oppressive Knowledge Production," *Curriculum Inquiry* 43, no. 4 (2013): 426.
10. Ibid., 430.
11. One exception to this is institutions of higher education. Colleges and universities have unquestionably been essential to most Queer of Color scholarship.
12. Woodrow Wilson, "Special Statement," in *Keeping Our Fighters Fit: For War and After* by Edward Frank Allen (New York: The Century Co, 1918).
13. *High Schools and Sex Education: A Manuel of Suggestions on Education Related to Sex*, ed. by Benjamin C. Gruenberg (Washington: Government Printing Office, 1922), v.
14. Ibid.
15. Ferguson, *Aberrations in Black*, 1–2.
16. Stallings, *Funk the Erotic*, 16.
17. José Esteban Muñoz, *Cruising Utopia: The Then and There of Queer Futurity* (New York: New York University Press, 2009), 59.
18. Ibid.
19. Excellent and essential discussions of these issues beyond the exclusive borders of the United States include Judith Walkowitz's work on sex work in Victorian Britain, Kamala Kempadoo and Amalia L. Cabezas's work on sex work in the Caribbean, and Elizabeth Bernstein's research on the complexities of modern sex work around the world.
20. Ruth Rosen, *Lost Sisterhood: Prostitution in America, 1900-1918* (Baltimore: Johns Hopkins University Press, 1983), 1.
21. Ibid.
22. Ibid. Importantly, Foucault's *History of Sexuality*, Vol. 1 details the prevalence of this approach to individual deviancy and the reasons for its decline.
23. Ibid., 2.
24. I speak of abolition in quotation marks to honor the ways in which we are still grappling with the socioeconomic and political ramifications of slavery's existence today.
25. Cynthia Blair, *I've Got to Make My Livin': Black Women's Sex Work in Turn-of-the-Century Chicago* (Chicago: University of Chicago Press, 2010), 4.

26 Ibid., 20.
27 Rosen, *Lost Sisterhood*, 4.
28 Ibid., xiii, xvii.
29 See Alex Smolak, "White Slavery, Whorehouse Riots, Venereal Disease, and Saving Women: Historical Context of Prostitution Interventions and Harm Reduction in New York City during the Progressive Era," *Social Work in Public Health* 28 (2013): 496–508.
30 Mara L. Keire, *For Business or Pleasure* (Baltimore: Johns Hopkins University Press, 2010), 24.
31 Ibid., 46.
32 Rosen, *Lost Sisterhood*, 31.
33 Ibid., 46.
34 Blair, *I've Got to Make My Livin'*, 4.
35 Ibid., 38.
36 Ibid., 44.
37 Even the term "agency" needs to be understood as limited here, as it is deeply tied to notions of humanity that always already restricted prostitutes from inclusion; prostitutes could only be seen as lacking agency because their activities were understood as inhuman.
38 Blair, *I've Got to Make My Livin'*, 48.
39 Keire, *For Business or Pleasure*, 7.
40 Ibid., 8.
41 Ibid.
42 Ibid., 51.
43 Ibid., 52.
44 Ibid.
45 Ibid.
46 Ibid.
47 Ibid., 57.
48 Ibid., 62.
49 Blair, *I've Got to Make My Livin'*, 7.
50 Ibid., 68.
51 Rosen, *Lost Sisterhood*, 6.
52 Keire, *For Business or Pleasure*, 68.
53 Blair, *I've Got to Make My Livin'*, 6.
54 Ferguson, *Aberrations in Black*, 41.
55 Rosen, *Lost Sisterhood*, 13.
56 Jensen, *Dirty Words*, 21.

57 Ibid.
58 Keire, *For Business or Pleasure*, 88.
59 Rosen, *Lost Sisterhood*, 21.
60 Ibid., 21–3.
61 Ibid., 21–2.
62 Jennifer Terry, *An American Obsession: Science, Medicine, and Homosexuality in Modern Society* (Chicago: University of Chicago Press, 1999), 82.
63 Ibid.
64 Ibid.
65 Keire, *For Business or Pleasure*, 90.
66 Rosen, *Lost Sisterhood*, 32.
67 Ibid., 19.
68 Jensen, *Dirty Words*, 76.
69 Keire, *For Business or Pleasure*, 105.
70 Ibid.
71 Ibid.
72 Ibid., 106.
73 Jensen, *Dirty Words*, 80–1.
74 Ibid., 81.
75 Keire, *For Business or Pleasure*, 108.
76 Jensen, *Dirty Words*, xii, 9.
77 Keire, *For Business or Pleasure*, 109.
78 Ibid., 111.
79 Ibid., 111–12.
80 Rosen, *Lost Sisterhood*, 15.
81 Ibid., 113; Also see Carole Vance's work in "Innocence and Experience: Melodramatic Narratives of Sex Trafficking and Their Consequences for Law and Policy" for a crucial breakdown of the relationship between sex trafficking and melodrama.
82 Keire, *For Business or Pleasure*, 70.
83 Ibid.
84 Ibid., 72.
85 Ferguson, *Aberrations in Black*, 39.
86 Nicole F. Bromfield, "Sex Slavery and Sex Trafficking of Women in the United States: Historical and Contemporary Parallels, Policies, and Perspectives in Social Work," *Affilia: Journal of Women and Social Work* 3 (1): 130.
87 Keire, *For Business or Pleasure*, 75.
88 Rosen, *Lost Sisterhood*, 118.
89 Ibid., 133.

90   Ibid.
91   Jensen, *Dirty Words*, 12.
92   Rosen, *Lost Sisterhood*, 119.
93   Ibid., 121.
94   Ibid., 122.
95   Judy Yung, *Unbound Feet: A Social History of Chinese Women in San Francisco* (Berkeley: University of California Press, 1995), 26.
96   Ibid., 27.
97   Ibid., 28.
98   Ibid.
99   Ibid.
100 Ibid., 31.
101 Ibid.
102 Ibid., 71.
103 Ibid., 73.
104 Ibid., 76.
105 Ibid.
106 Blair, *I've Got to Make My Livin'*, 10.
107 Keire, *For Business or Pleasure*, 88.
108 Dorothy Roberts, *Killing the Black Body: Race, Reproduction, and the Meaning of Liberty* (New York: Vintage, 1998), 8.
109 Ibid.
110 Canada has garnered different attention by scholars of sex education on this point, as it has been more readily impacted by the widespread activist work being done by indigenous groups within the country to ensure the inclusion of indigenous knowledge and experience in the crafting of national comprehensive sex education policies and curriculum.
111 Sarah Deer, *The Beginning and End of Rape: Confronting Sexual Violence in Native America* (Minneapolis: University of Minnesota Press, 2015), 62.
112 See the work of Vine Deloria Jr. and K. Tsianina Lomawamia for particularly through and compelling discussions of the experience of Native children in boarding schools at this time.
113 Deer, *The Beginning and End of Rape*, 71.
114 Ibid., 69.
115 Rosen, *Lost Sisterhood*, 16.
116 Ibid.
117 "Maya Angelou: Gather Together in My Name" interview posted by the Visionary Project on January 29, 2010, https://www.youtube.com/watch?v=59cS6TO4IdQ.

Chapter 2

1. Sylvia Rivera, interview with Leslie Feinberg from 1988, cited in: https://www.nswp.org/timeline/event/street-transvestite-action-revolutionaries-found-star-house.
2. Maria Lugones, "Heterosexualism and the Colonial/Modern Gender System," *Hypatia* 22, no. 1 (Winter 2007): 189.
3. Tompkins, "Intersections of Race, Gender, and Sexuality," 173.
4. Ibid.
5. Aníbal Quijano, "Coloniality of Power, Eurocentrism and Latin America," *Nepantla: Views from the South* 1, no. 3 (2000): 537.
6. Ferguson, *Aberrations in Black*, viii.
7. Siobhan Somerville, *Queering the Color Line: Race and the Invention of Homosexuality in American Culture* (Durham and London: Duke University Press, 2000), 137.
8. Adrienne Davis, "'Don't Let Nobody Bother Yo' Principle': The Sexual Economy of American Slavery," in *Sister Circle: Black Women and Work*, ed. by S. Harley (New Brunswick: Rutgers University Press, 2002), 103–27, 104.
9. Ibid., 117.
10. Cedric Robinson, *Black Marxism: The Making of the Black Radical Tradition* (Chapel Hill and London: The University of North Carolina Press, 2000), 109.
11. Ibid., 129.
12. Ibid., 178.
13. Ibid., 10.
14. Ferguson, *Aberrations in Black*, 20.
15. Kathi Weeks, *The Problem with Work* (Durham and London: Duke University Press, 2011), 42.
16. Ibid., 44.
17. Ibid., 45.
18. Ibid., 50.
19. Ferguson, *Aberrations in Black*, 11.
20. Ibid., 104.
21. US Congress, Senate, *Omnibus Budget Reconciliation Act of 1981*, 97th Congress, 1981, H.R. 3982, 579. https://www.congress.gov/bill/97th-congress/house-bill/3982/text. It was then subsumed under Title XX of Subtitle G of the Public Health Service Act and renamed the Adolescent Family Life Demonstration Project.
22. US Senate Committee Print of the Senate Special Committee, *Legislative History of the Omnibus Budget Reconciliation Act of 1981* (August 13, 1981), 579.

23 US Senate, 98th Congress. 2nd Session. No. 98-496, *The Adolescent Family Life Act* (Washington: Government Printing Office, 1984), 7.
24 Ibid., 4.
25 Ibid., 8.
26 Terry, *An American Obsession*, 79.
27 Roberts, *Killing the Black Body*, 17, 156.
28 Ibid., 17.
29 Lord, *Condom Nation*, 143.
30 US Senate, *Social Security Act*, http://www.ssa.gov/OP_Home/ssact/title05/0510.htm (accessed April 27, 2014).
31 US House of Representatives, "Committee on Energy and Commerce," in *Extension of Funding for Abstinence Education* (Washington: Government Printing Office, 2002), 3.
32 SIECUS, "A History of Federal Funding for Abstinence-Only-Until Marriage Programs," http://www.siecus.org/in dex.cfm?fuseaction=page.viewPage&pageID=1340&nodeID=1.
33 Roberts, *Killing the Black Body*, 18.
34 Charles Keckner, "DHHS Abstinence Education Programs." US House of Representatives: Committee on Oversight and Government Reform, 2008, http://www.hhs.gov/asl/testify/2008/04/t20080423a.html.
35 Roberts, *Killing the Black Body*, 18.
36 US Congress, Senate, *Patient Protection and Affordable Care Act 2009*, HR 3590, 347.
37 Ibid., 599.
38 Ibid., 603–4.
39 Ibid., 602–5.
40 Nancy Kendall, *The Sex Education Debates* (Chicago: The University of Chicago Press, 2013), 226–7.
41 See: Janice Irving, "Doing It with Words: Discourse and the Sex Education Culture Wars," *Critical Inquiry* 27, no. 1 (Autumn 2000): 58–76; and Janice Irving, *Talk about Sex: The Battles over Sex Education in the United States* (Berkeley: University of California Press, 2002).
42 Kendall, *The Sex Education Debates*, 610.
43 SIECUS, "A History of Federal Funding for Abstinence-Only-Until Marriage Programs," 7.
44 42 US Code 710—Sexual Risk Avoidance Education.
45 Ibid.
46 Ibid.

47 Elizabeth Bernstein, *Temporarily Yours: Intimacy, Authenticity, and the Commerce of Sex* (Chicago: The University of Chicago Press, 2007), 48.

Chapter 3

1 Carmen Hayes, in *A Taste for Brown Sugar: Black Women in Pornography*, by Mirelle Miller-Young (Durham: Duke University Press, 2014).
2 Ferguson, *Aberrations in Black*, ix.
3 Ibid.
4 Andrea Smith, "Heteropatriarchy and the Three Pillars of White Supremacy: Rethinking Women of Color Organizing," in *Color of Violence* (Boston: South End Press, 2006), 72.
5 Lugones, "Heterosexualism and the Colonial/Modern Gender System," 188.
6 Fosdick, "The Commission on Training Camp Activities," 824.
7 Morrow, "Prophylaxis of Social Diseases," 28.
8 *High Schools and Sex Education*, by Gruenberg, 2.
9 Sara Ahmed, *Queer Phenomenology* (Durham and London: Duke University Press, 2006), 50.
10 Ibid., 57.
11 Ibid., 49.
12 Ibid., 92.
13 Ibid., 91.
14 Ibid., 113.
15 Ibid., 114.
16 Ibid., 116.
17 Ibid., 140.
18 Ibid., 107.
19 Paulo Freire, *Pedagogy of the Oppressed: 30th Anniversary Edition*, trans. by Myra Bergman Ramos (New York: Bloomsburg, 2000), 57.
20 Ibid., 47.
21 Ibid., 50.
22 Ibid., 51.
23 Sylvia Wynter, "Afterword: 'Beyond Miranda's Meanings: Un/silencing the "Demonic Ground" of Caliban's 'Woman,'"" in *Out of the Kumbla: Caribbean Women and Literature*, ed. by Carole Boyce Davies and Elaine Savory Fido (Trenton: Africa World Press, Inc., 1990), 362–3.
24 Foucault, "Governmentality," 103.

25 Ibid., 100.
26 Ibid., 103.
27 Michel Foucault, "The Political Technology of Individuals," in *Technologies of the Self: A Seminar with Michel Foucault*, ed. by Luther H. Martin, Huck Gutman, and Patrick H. Hutton (Amherst: University of Massachusetts Press, 1988), 152.
28 See his discussion of biopolitics in History of Sexuality, Vol. 1 and his lecture, "The Birth of Biopolitics," for more details on this term.
29 David Archard, "How Should We Teach Sex?" *Journal of Philosophy of Education* 32, no. 3 (1998): 437.
30 Amy Gutmann, "Democracy and Democratic Education," *Studies in Philosophy of Education* 12 (1993): 1.
31 Ibid., 110.
32 Josh Corngold, "Misplaced Priorities: Gutmann's Democratic Theory, Children's Autonomy, and Sex Education Policy," *Studies in Philosophy of Education* 30 (2011): 68.
33 Josh Corngold, "Moral Pluralism and Sex Education," *Educational Theory* 65, no. 5 (2013): 470–1, 477–82.
34 Paula McAvoy, "The Aims of Sex Education: Demoting Autonomy and Promoting Mutuality," *Educational Theory* 65, no. 5 (2013): 487.
35 Ibid.
36 Ibid., 492.
37 Lauren Bialystok, "'My Child, My Choice?,' Mandatory curriculum, Sex, and the Conscience of Parents," *Educational Theory* 68, no. 1 (2018): 27.
38 Cris Mayo, *Disputing the Subject of Sex* (Lanham: Rowman and Littlefield Publishers, Inc., 2004), 4.
39 Ibid., 10.
40 Cris Mayo, "Gagged and Bound: Sex Education, Secondary Virginity, and the Welfare Reform Act," *Philosophy of Education* (1998): 311–15. See also: Cris Mayo, "Unsettled Relations: Schools, Gay Marriage, and Educating for Sexuality," *Educational Theory* 65, no. 5 (2013): 544, and Cris Mayo, "Performance Anxiety: Sexuality and School Controversy," *Philosophy of Education* (1996): 281.
41 Cris Mayo, "Disruptions of Desire: From Androgynes to Genderqueer," *Philosophy of Education* (2007): 50.
42 Deborah P. Britzman, *The Very Thought of Education: Psychoanalysis and the Impossible Professions* (Albany: SUNY Press, 2009), 38.
43 Ibid.
44 Jen Gilbert, *Sexuality in School: The Limits of Education* (Minneapolis: University of Minnesota Press, 2014), 85.

45 Mayo, "Performance Anxiety," 31.
46 Michelle Fine and Sarah I. McClelland, "Sexuality Education and Desire: Still Missing after All These Years," *Harvard Educational Review* 76, no. 3 (Fall 2006): 300.
47 Louise Allen and Moira Carmody, "'Pleasure has no passport': Re-visiting the Potential of Pleasure in Sexuality Education," *Sex Education* 12, no. 4 (2012): 455.
48 Louisa Allen, "Denying the Sexual Subject," *British Educational Research Journal* 33, no. 2 (2007): 228.
49 Vanessa Cameron-Lewis and Louisa Allen, "Teaching Pleasure *and* Danger in Sexuality Education," *Sexuality, Society and Learning* 13, no. 2 (2013): 123.
50 Kendall, *The Sex Education Debates*, 236.
51 Dank, et al. "Estimating the Size and Structure of the Underground Commercial Sex Economy in Eight Major US Cities," *The Urban Institute*, March 2014, 134.

Chapter 4

1 Kaniya Walker, "To Protect Black Trans Lives, Decriminalize Sex Work," https://www.aclu.org/news/lgbt-rights/to-protect-black-trans-lives-decriminalize-sex-work/.
2 Jake Alimahomed-Wilson and Dana Williams, "State Violence, Social Control, and Resistance," *Journal of Social Justice* 6 (2016): 5.
3 Chandan Reddy, *Freedom with Violence* (Durham: Duke University Press, 2011), 20.
4 Ibid., 38.
5 UNESCO, "UN urges Comprehensive Approach to Sexuality Education," October 1, 2018, https://unesdoc. unesco.org/ark:/48223/pf0000260770.
6 Leslie M. Kantor, Lori Rolleri, and Katherine Kolios, "Doug Kirby's Contribution to the Field of Sex Education," *Sex Education* 14, no. 5 (2014): 473–80.
7 Alessandra Aresu, "Sex Education in Modern and Contemporary China: Interrupted Debates across the Last Century," *International Journal of Educational Development* 29 (2009): 536.
8 Ibid., 533.
9 Sara Wu, "Revised Chinese Law Sparks Debate on Sexuality Education," *Reuters*, October 25, 2020, https://www.reuters.com/article/china-society-education-sex/revised-chinese-law-sparks-debate-on-sexuality-education-idUSL4N2HG01X.

10 Jinping Lyu, Xiaoyun Shen, and Therese Hesketh, "Sexual Knowledge, Attitudes and Behaviors among Undergraduate Students in China—Implications for Sex Education," *International Journal of Environmental Research and Public Health* 17, no. 18: 6716.
11 Jeremy Shiffman et al., "International Norms and the Politics of Sexuality Education in Nigeria," *Globalization and Health* 14, no. 63 (2018). From https://globalizationandhealth.biomedcentral.com/articles/10.1186/s12992-018-0377-2.
12 Ibid.
13 "Brazil Sex Education Material Suspended by President," *BBC News*, May 25, 2011, https://www.bbc.com/news/world-latin-america-13554077 (accessed March 14, 2021).
14 Brazilian Committee Specialized in Sexology of FEBRASGO and Brazilian Association of Studies on Human Sexuality, "Sexuality Education in Schools," December 2018, http://www.scielo.br/scielo.php?script=sci_arttext&pid=S0100-72032018001200731.
15 Catherine Osborn, "Brazil Reduces Sex Education Amid Spike in Sexually Transmitted Infections," November 15, 2019, https://www.pri.org/stories/2019-11-15/brazil-reduces-sex-education-amid-spike-sexually-transmitted-infections.
16 Ernesto Londono and Leticia Casado, "Brazil Under Bolsonaro Has Message for Teenagers: Save Sex for Marriage," reported in the *New York Times*, January 16, 2020, https://www.nytimes.com/2020/01/26/world/americas/brazil-teen-pregnancy-Bolsonaro.html.
17 Jonathan Zimmerman's *Too Hot to Handle* is perhaps the most prominent exception to this, though his research is differently oriented than what I am calling for here.
18 Yeon, Jung Yu, "The Moral Code of Chinese Sex Workers," *Sapiens*, 2017, https://www.sapiens.org/culture/china-sex-trade-moral-code/.
19 NSWA Homepage, https://www.nswp.org/featured/nigeria-sex-workers-association-precious-jewels.
20 Transgender Europe, "Trans Day of Visibility Press Release: Over 2,000 Trans People Killed in the Last 8 Years," March 30, 2016, https://tgeu.org/transgender-day-of-visibility-2016-trans-murder-monitoring-update/.
21 Amanda De Lisio and Michael Silk, "After the Olympics: Stories from Rio's Sex Workers," May 12, 2017, https://theconversation.com/after-the-olympics-stories-from-rios-sex-workers-73555.
22 Jasbir Puar, "Rethinking Homonationalism," in *Journal of Middle East Studies* 45, no. 2, (May 2013): 337.

23. Jasbir Puar, "Coda: The Cost of Getting Better: Suicide, Sensation, Switchpoints," in *GLQ: A Journal of Lesbian and Gay Studies* 18, no. 1, (2012): 153.
24. M. Jacqui Alexander, *Pedagogies of Crossing* (Durham and London: Duke University Press, 2006): 207–208.
25. Mark Unger, "State Violence and Lesbian, Gay, Bisexual and Transgender (lgbt) Rights," *New Political Science* 22, no. 1 (2000): 61.
26. Ibid.
27. Bernstein, *Temporarily Yours*, 7.
28. Ibid., 18.
29. Ibid., 7.
30. Ibid., 13–14.
31. Nancy A. Wonders and Raymond Michalowski, "Bodies, Borders, and Sex Tourism in a Globalized World: A Tale of Two Cities—Amsterdam and Havana," *Social Problems* 48, no. 4 Special Issue (November 2001): 545.
32. Ros Williams, "Postcolonial Discourses and 'Sex Tourism,'" https://www.e-ir.info/2011/08/15/postcolonial-discourses-and-sex-tourism/ (accessed June 2020).
33. Ibid., 3.
34. Kamala Kempadoo, *Sexing the Caribbean: Gender, Race and Sexual Labor* (New York: Routledge, 2004), 39.
35. Ibid.
36. Jillian Grouchy, "The Global Impact of the Sex Tourism Industry: Issues of Legalization," http://research.library.mun.ca/id/eprint/11816 (accessed June 2020), 3.
37. Ibid., 6.
38. Lauren Berlant, "Cruel Optimism," in *The Affect Theory Reader*, ed. by Melissa Gregg and Gregory J. Seigworth (Durham: Duke University Press, 2009), 93.
39. Ibid., 94.
40. Ibid.
41. "Empower's Education . . . Learning by Doing," *Empower Foundation of Thailand*, http://www.empowerfound ation.org/e ducation_en.html.

Chapter 5

1. Margo St. James, Hooker's Ball 1974. https://diva.sfsu.edu/collections/sfbatv/bundles/191566.
2. For a thorough and compelling justification of the "productive" nature of critique, or, rather, productivity's dependence on critique, see Mathias Thaler's

"Unhinged Frames: Assessing Thought Experiments in Normative Political Theory," *British Journal of Political Science* 48 (2016): 1119–41.
3   Ahmed, *Queer Phenomenology*, 91–2.
4   Wanda Pillow, "Bodies are Dangerous: Using Feminist Genealogy as Policy Studies Methodology," *Journal of Education Policy* 18, no. 2 (2003): 146.
5   Stefano Harney and Fred Moten, *The Undercommons: Fugitive Planning and Black Study* (Wivenhoe: Minor Compositions, 2013), 76.
6   Ibid., 77.
7   Ibid., 74.
8   See Erica Meiners, *For the Children? Protecting Innocence in a Carceral State* (Minneapolis: University of Minnesota Press, 2016) for an excellent discussion of these tensions.
9   Bradley A. U. Levinson, Margaret Sutton, and Teresa Winstead, "Education Policy as a Practice of Power," *Educational Policy* 23, no. 6 (November 2009): 767.
10 Ibid., 769.
11 Ibid., 778–9.
12 Reddy, *Freedom with Violence*, 204.
13 Maxine Greene, *Releasing the Imagination* (San Francisco: Jossey-Bass Inc. Publishers, 1995), 21.
14 Ibid., 19.
15 Ibid., 28–32.
16 Ibid., 19.
17 Ibid., 22.
18 Henry Giroux, *The Violence of Organized Forgetting: Thinking Beyond America's Disimagination Machine* (San Francisco: City Light Books, 2014), 497.
19 Robin D. G. Kelley, *Freedom Dreams: The Black Radical Imagination* (Boston: Beacon Press, 2002), 2.
20 Ibid.
21 Ibid., 2–3.
22 Phillip Brian Harper, "The Evidence of Felt Intuition: Minority Experience, Everyday Life, and Critical Speculative Knowledge," *GLQ* 6, no. 4 (2000): 649.
23 Ibid., 650.
24 Of course, the affective is not itself inherently immune to such logics. Many scholars, including Sara Ahmed and Lauren Berlant, have clearly described how affect can be just as much a tool for normativity than it can be for resistance. In attaching affect to a set of utopian demands, following Weeks, that explicitly resist some of these normative processes, I hope to show that such a view of affective experience might enact that resistance.

25 Kelley, *Freedom Dreams*, 5–6.
26 Ibid., 9–10.
27 Boggs in Kelley, *Freedom Dreams*, 133–4.
28 Weeks, *The Problem with Work*, 186.
29 Ibid., 194–7; the "new that is familiar" is a phrase Weeks takes from Ernst Bloch's work.
30 Ibid., 197.
31 Ibid., 202.
32 Ibid., 203.
33 Ibid., 207–8.
34 Ibid., 220.
35 Lisa Duggan and José Esteban Muñoz, "Hope and Hopelessness: A Dialogue," *Women & Performance: A Journal of Feminist Theory* 19, no. 2 (July 2009): 275.
36 Ibid., 276.
37 Sara Ahmed, *The Promise of Happiness* (Durham and London: Duke University Press, 2010), 59.
38 Duggan and Muñoz, "Hope and Hopelessness," 278.
39 Ibid., 281.
40 Both Kelley and Weeks can rightfully be seen as aligned with humanist intentions, which may point to an inherent contradiction between my own use of these scholars as if they are themselves seamlessly aligned. I think that Muñoz's use of educated hope offers a way of doing some of the work Kelley and Weeks desire while remaining skeptical of the norms to which hope can attach itself.
41 José Esteban Muñoz, "Theorizing Queer Inhumanisms: The Sense of Brownness," *GLQ* 21, nos. 2–3 (2005): 209.
42 Sianne Ngai, *Ugly Feelings* (Cambridge, MA: Harvard University Press, 2007), 4.
43 Ibid., 3.
44 Ibid., 261.
45 Ibid., 270.
46 Ibid., 271.
47 Ibid., 284.
48 Ibid.
49 Ibid., 297.
50 Ibid.
51 See Christina Sharpe, *In the Wake: On Blackness and Being* (Durham: Duke University Press, 2016). I take seriously the many ways that Sharpe defines, plays with, feels through and with and in, and theorizes the wake, especially as it relates to practices of care, relations to death, and new forms of knowledge production, and I hope to invoke them all.

52 Harney and Moten, *The Undercommons*, 19.
53 Ibid., 18.

Conclusion

1   Nnedi Okorafor, *Binti* (Tor Books, 2015), 13.
2   Ibid., 31.
3   Ibid., 29.
4   Ibid., 65.
5   Meiners's use of "not this" is derived from her study of Elizabeth Povenelli's discussion of resistance in late liberalism.
6   Miller-Brown, *A Taste of Brown Sugar*, 51.
7   June Jordan, "A New Politics of Sexuality," *Transformations: Feminist Pathways to Global Change* (2015): 133.
8   Alexis Pauline Gumbs, in *Octavia's Brood*, 34.
9   Harney and Moten, *The Undercommons*, 20.
10 CeCe McDonald, interview with Alok Vaid-Menon with Lambda Literary, 2015.
11 Kathrine McKittrick, *Sylvia Wynter: On Being Human as Praxis* (Durham and London: Duke University Press, 2015), xxiv.
12 Missy Elliot—"Work It."
13 Whalidah Imarisha, *Octavia's Brood*, Introduction, 3.
14 Janet Gonzalez, in Laura E. Enriquez, "Multigenerational Punishment: Shared Experiences of Undocumented Immigration Status Within Mixed-Status Families," *Journal of Marriage and Family* 77 (2015): 945.
15 Ursula Le Guin, *The Left Hand of Darkness* (New York: Ace Books, 1969): 96.
16 Zakiyyah Iman Jackson, "Outer Worlds: The Persistence of Race in Movement 'Beyond the Human,'" *GLQ: A Journal of Lesbian and Gay Studies* 21, nos. 2–3 (June 2015): 215.
17 Stallings, *Funk the Erotic*, xv.
18 Harney and Moten, *The Undercommons*, 26.
19 Tobin Siebers, "A Sexual Culture for Disabled People," *Sex and disability* 17, no. 8 (2012):42.
20 Microsoft Word wanted *me* to know, as I typed the word "slutty," that "This language may be offensive to your reader." I want *you* to know that I meant what I said.
21 Ditto, but about "whore."

Bibliography

Ahmed, Sara. *Living a Feminist Life*. Durham and London: Duke University Press, 2017.

Ahmed, Sara. *The Promise of Happiness*. Durham and London: Duke University Press, 2010.

Ahmed, Sara. *Queer Phenomenology*. Durham and London: Duke University Press, 2006.

Alexander, M. Jacqui. *Pedagogies of Crossing: Meditations on Feminism, Sexual Politics, Memory, and the Sacred*. Durham and London: Duke University Press, 2005.

Alimahomed-Wilson, Jake and Dana Williams. "State Violence, Social Control, and Resistance." *Journal of Social Justice* 6 (2016): 1–15.

Allen, Louisa. "Denying the Sexual Subject." *British Educational Research Journal* 33, no. 2 (2007): 221–34.

Allen, Louise and Moira Carmody. "'Pleasure has no passport': Re-visiting the Potential of Pleasure in Sexuality Education." *Sex Education* 12, no. 4 (2012): 455–68.

Archard, David. "How Should We Teach Sex?" *Journal of Philosophy of Education* 32, no. 3 (1998): 437–49.

Aresu, Alessandra. "Sex Education in Modern and Contemporary China: Interrupted Debates across the Last Century." *International Journal of Educational Development* 29 (2009): 532–41.

Berlant, Lauren. "Cruel Optimism." In *The Affect Theory Reader*, edited by Melissa Gregg and Gregory J. Seigworth, 93–117. Durham: Duke University Press, 2009.

Bernstein, Elizabeth. *Temporarily Yours: Intimacy, Authenticity, and the Commerce of Sex*. Chicago: The University of Chicago Press, 2007.

Bialystok, Lauren. "'My Child, My Choice?', Mandatory Curriculum, Sex, and the Conscience of Parents." *Educational Theory* 68, no. 1 (2018): 11–29

Blair, Cynthia. *I've Got to Make My Livin': Black Women's Sex Work in Turn-of-the-Century Chicago*. Chicago: University of Chicago Press, 2010.

"Brazil Sex Education Material Suspended by President," *BBC News*, May 25, 2011. https://www.bbc.com/news/world-latin-america-13554077.

Brazilian Committee Specialized in Sexology of FEBRASGO and Brazilian Association of Studies on Human Sexuality. "Sexuality Education in Schools,"

December 2018, http://www.scielo.br/scielo.php?script=sci_arttext&pid=S0100-72032018001200731.

Britzman, Deborah. "Precocious Education." In *Thinking Queer: Sexuality, Culture, and Education*, edited by Susan Talbert and Shirley R. Steinberg, 33–59. New York: Peter Lang, 2000.

Brockenbrough, ed. "Introduction to the Special Issue: Queers of Color and Anti-Oppressive Knowledge Production." *Curriculum Inquiry* 43, no. 4 (2013): 426–40.

Bromfield, Nicole F. "Sex Slavery and Sex Trafficking of Women in the United States: Historical and Contemporary Parallels, Policies, and Perspectives in Social Work." *Affilia: Journal of Women and Social Work* 3 (1): 129–39.

Butler, Octavia. *Parable of the Sower*. New York: Four Walls Eight Windows, 1993.

Cameron-Lewis, Vanessa and Lousia Allen. "Teaching Pleasure *and* Danger in Sexuality Education." *Sexuality, Society and Learning* 13, no. 2 (2013): 121–32.

Carter, Julian B. "Birds, Bees, and Venereal Disease: Toward an Intellectual History of Sex Education." *Journal of the History of Sexuality* 2, no. 2 (2001): 213–49.

Cohen, Cathy J. "Deviance and Resistance." *Du Bois Review: Social Science Research on Race* 1, no. 1 (2004): 27–45.

Cohen, Cathy J. "Punks, Bulldaggers, and Welfare Queens: The Radical Potential of Queer Politics?" *GLQ: A Journal of Lesbian and Gay Studies* 3 (1997): 21–51.

Corngold, Josh. "Misplaced Priorities: Gutmann's Democratic Theory, Children's Autonomy, and Sex Education Policy." *Studies in Philosophy of Education* 30 (2011): 67–84.

Corngold, Josh. "Moral Pluralism and Sex Education." *Educational Theory* 65, no. 5 (2013): 462–82.

Dank, Meridith L., P. Mitchell Downey, Cybele Kotonias, Deborah Mayer, Colleen Owens, Laura Pacifici, and Lilly Yu. "Estimating the Size and Structure of the Underground Commercial Sex Economy in Eight Major US Cities," *The Urban Institute*, March 2014.

Davis, Adrienne. 2002. "'Don't Let Nobody Bother Yo' Principle': The Sexual Economy of American Slavery." In *Sister Circle: Black Women and Work*, edited by S. Harley, 103–27. New Brunswick: Rutgers University Press.

Deer, Sarah. *The Beginning and End of Rape: Confronting Sexual Violence in Native America*. Minneapolis: University of Minnesota Press, 2015.

De Lisio, Amanda and Michael Silk. "After the Olympics: Stories from Rio's Sex Workers." Published May 12, 2017. https://theconversation.com/after-the-olympics-stories-from-rios-sex-workers-73555.

Duggan, Lisa and José Esteban Muñoz. "Hope and Hopelessness: A Dialogue." *Women & Performance: A Journal of Feminist Theory* 19, no. 2 (July 2009): 275–83.

Ferguson, Roderick. *Aberrations in Black: Toward A Queer of Color Critique.* Minneapolis: University of Minnesota Press, 2003.

Fine, Michelle and Sarah I. McClelland. "Sexuality Education and Desire: Still Missing after All These Years." *Harvard Educational Review* 76, no. 3 (Fall 2006): 297–338.

Fosdick, Raymond B. "The Commission on Training Camp Activities." *Proceedings of the Academy of Political Science in the City of New York* 7, no. 4 (February 1918). *Social Sciences Index Retrospective: 1929-1983 (H.W. Wilson).* EBSCOhost. Accessed April 10, 2014.

Foucault, Michel. *Ethics: Subjectivity and Truth.* Edited by Paul Rabinow. Translated by Robert Hurley and others. New York: W.W. Norton & Co., Inc., 1994.

Foucault, Michel. "Governmentality." In *The Foucault Effect: Studies in Governmentality,* edited by Graham Burchell, Colin Gordon and Peter Miller. Chicago: The University of Chicago Press, 1991.

Foucault, Michel. *The History of Sexuality,* vol. 1. New York: Pantheon Books, 1978.

Foucault, Michel. "Nietzsche, Genealogy, History." In *Language, Counter-Memory, Practice: Selected Essays and Interviews,* edited by D. F. Bouchard, 139–64. Ithaca: Cornell University Press, 1977.

Foucault, Michel. "The Political Technology of Individuals." In *Technologies of the Self: A Seminar with Michel Foucault,* edited by Luther H. Martin, Huck Gutman, and Patrick H. Hutton, 16–49. Amherst: University of Massachusetts Press, 1988.

Foucault, Michel. "Sex, Power and the Politics of Identity." In *Essential Works of Foucault 1954-1984,* edited by Paul Rabinow, 163–73. Harmondsworth: Penguin Books, 2000.

Foucault, Michel. "The Subject and Power." *Critical Inquiry* 8, no. 4 (Summer 1982): 777–95.

Freire, Paulo. *Pedagogy of the Oppressed: 30th Anniversary Edition.* Translated by Myra Bergman Ramos. New York: Bloomsburg, 2000.

Gilbert, Jen. *Sexuality in School: The Limits of Education.* Minneapolis: University of Minnesota Press, 2014.

Giroux, Henry. *The Violence of Organize Forgetting: Thinking Beyond America's Disimagination Machine.* San Francisco: City Lights Books, 2014.

Greene, Maxine. *Releasing the Imagination.* San Francisco: Jossey-Bass Inc., Publishers, 1995.

Grouchy, Jillian. "The Global Impact of the Sex Tourism Industry: Issues of Legalization." Accessed June 2020. http://research.library.mun.ca/id/eprint/11816.

Gumbs, Alexis Pauline. "Evidence." In *Octavia's Brood,* edited by Walidah Imarisha, 33–42. Oakland: AK Press, 2015.

Gutmann, Amy. "Democracy and Democratic Education." *Studies in Philosophy of Education* 12 (1993): 1–9.

Hall, Stuart. "When Was 'The Post-Colonial'? Thinking at the Limit." In *The Post-Colonial Question*, edited by Iain Chambers and Lidia Curti, 242–60. New York: Routledge, 1996.

Harney, Stefano and Fred Moten. *The Undercommons: Fugitive Planning and Black Study*. Wivenhoe: Minor Compositions, 2013.

Harper, Phillip Brian. "The Evidence of Felt Intuition: Minority Experience, Everyday Life, and Critical Speculative Knowledge." *GLQ* 6, no. 4 (2000): 621–59.

High Schools and Sex Education: A Manuel of Suggestions on Education Related to Sex. Edited by Benjamin C. Gruenberg. Washington: Government Printing Office, 1922.

"A History of Federal Funding for Abstinence-Only-Until Marriage Programs." *SIECUS*, http://www.siecus.org/in dex.cfm?fuseaction=page.viewPage&pageID=1340&nodeID=1.

Huber, Valarie J. and Michael W. Firmin. "A History of Sex Education in the United States Since 1900." *International Journal of Educational Reform* 23, no. 1 (2014): 25–51.

Irvine, Janice. "Doing It with Words: Discourse and the Sex Education Culture Wars." *Critical Inquiry* 27, no. 1 (Autumn 2000): 58–76.

Irvine, Janice. *Talk about Sex: The Battles over Sex Education in the United States*. Berkeley: University of California Press, 2002.

Jackson, Zakiyyah Iman. "Outer Worlds: The Persistence of Race in Movement 'Beyond the Human.'" *GLQ: A Journal of Lesbian and Gay Studies* 21, nos. 2–3 (June 2015): 215–18.

Jenness, Valarie. "From Sex as Sin to Sex as Work: COYOTE and the Reorganization of Prostitution as a Social Problem." *Social Problems* 37, no. 3 (August 1990): 403–20.

Jensen, Robin. *Dirty Words: The Rhetoric of Public Sex Education, 1870–1924*. Champaign: University of Illinois Press, 2010.

Kantor, Leslie M., Lori Rolleri, and Katherine Kolios. "Doug Kirby's Contribution to the Field of Sex Education." *Sex Education* 14, no. 5 (2014): 473–80.

Keckner, Charles. "DHHS Abstinence Education Programs." http://www.hhs.gov/asl/testify/2008/04/t20080423a.html.

Keire, Mara L. *For Business or Pleasure*. Baltimore: Johns Hopkins University Press, 2010.

Kelley, Robin D. G. *Freedom Dreams: The Black Radical Imagination*. Boston: Beacon Press, 2002.

Kempadoo, Kamala. *Sexing the Caribbean: Gender, Race and Sexual Labor*. New York: Routledge, 2004.

Kendall, Nancy. *The Sex Education Debates*. Chicago: The University of Chicago Press, 2013.

Koopman, Colin. *Genealogy as Critique: Foucault and the Problems of Modernity*. Bloomington: Indiana University Press, 2013.

Le Guin, Ursula. *The Left Hand of Darkness*. New York: Ace Books, 1969.

Levinson, Bradley A. U., Margaret Sutton, and Teresa Winstead. "Education Policy as a Practice of Power." *Educational Policy* 23, no. 6 (November 2009): 767–95.

Londono, Ernesto and Leticia Casado. "Brazil Under Bolsonaro Has Message for Teenagers: Save Sex for Marriage," reported in the *New York Times*, January 16, 2020. https://www.nytimes.com/2020/01/26/world/americas/brazil-teen-pregnancy-Bolsonaro.html.

Lord, Alexandra. *Condom Nation*. Baltimore: The Johns Hopkins University Press, 2010.

Lorde, Audre. "Poetry Is Not a Luxury." In *Sister Outsider: Essays and Speeches*, 36–9. New York: Ten Speed Press, 1984.

Lugones, Maria. "Heterosexualism and the Colonial/Modern Gender System." *Hypatia* 22, no. 1 (Winter 2007): 186–209.

Lyu, Jinping, Xiaoyun Shen, and Therese Hesketh. "Sexual Knowledge, Attitudes and Behaviors among Undergraduate Students in China – Implications for Sex Education." *International Journal of Environmental Research and Public Health* 17, no. 18 (2011): 1–7.

Mayo, Cris. *Disputing the Subject of Sex*. Lanham: Rowman and Littlefield Publishers, Inc., 2004.

Mayo, Cris. "Disruptions of Desire: From Androgynes to Genderqueer." *Philosophy of Education* (2007): 49–58.

Mayo, Cris. "Gagged and Bound: Sex Education, Secondary Virginity, and the Welfare Reform Act." *Philosophy of Education* (1998): 309–317.

Mayo, Cris. "Performance Anxiety: Sexuality and School Controversy." *Philosophy of Education* (1996): 281–9.

Mayo, Cris. "Unsettled Relations: Schools, Gay Marriage, and Educating for Sexuality." *Educational Theory* 65, no. 5 (2013): 544–58.

McAvoy, Paula. "The Aims of Sex Education: Demoting Autonomy and Promoting Mutuality." *Educational Theory* 65, no. 5 (2013): 483–95.

McKittrick, Kathrine. *Sylvia Wynter: On Being Human as Praxis*. Durham and London: Duke University Press, 2015.

Meiners, Erica. *For the Children? Protecting Innocence in a Carceral State*. Minneapolis: University of Minnesota Press, 2016.

Miller-Young, Mirelle. *A Taste for Brown Sugar*. Durham and London: Duke University Press, 2014.

Moran, Jeffrey. *Teaching Sex: The Shaping of Adolescence in the 20th Century.* Cambridge, MA: Harvard University Press, 2000.

Moraña, Mabel, Enrique Dussel, and Carlos A. Jáuregui. "Colonialism and it Replicants." In *Coloniality at Large: Latin America and the Postcolonial Debate,* edited by Mabel Moraña, Enrique Dussel, and Carlos A. Jáuregui, 1–22. Durham: Duke University Press, 2008.

Morrow, Prince A. "Prophylaxis of Social Diseases." *American Journal of Sociology* 13, no. 1 (July 1907): 20–33.

Muñoz, José Esteban. *Cruising Utopia: The Then and There of Queer Futurity.* New York: New York University Press, 2009.

Muñoz, José Esteban. "Theorizing Queer Inhumanism: The Sense of Brownness." *GLQ* 21, nos. 2–3 (2005): 209–10.

Ngai, Sianne. *Ugly Feelings.* Cambridge, MA: Harvard University Press, 2007.

Okorafor, Nnedi. *Binti.* Tordotcom, 2015.

Osborn, Catherine. "Brazil Reduces Sex Education amid Spike in Sexually Transmitted Infections." November 15, 2019. https://www.pri.org/stories/2019-11-15/brazil-reduces-sex-education-amid-spike-sexually-transmitted-infections.

Quijano, Anibal. "Coloniality of Power, Eurocentrism and Latin America." *Nepantla: Views from the South* 1, no. 3 (2000): 533–580.

Pillow, Wanda. "Bodies are Dangerous: Using feminist genealogy as policy studies methodology." *Journal of Education Policy* 18, no. 2 (2003): 145–59.

Puar, Jasbir. "Coda: The Cost of Getting Better: Suicide, Sensation, Switchpoints." *GLQ* 18, no. 1 (2012): 149–58.

Puar, Jasbir. "Rethinking Homonationalism." *International Journal of Middle East Studies* 45, no. 2 Special Issue (May 2013): 336–9.

Reddy, Chandan. *Freedom with Violence.* Durham: Duke University Press, 2011.

Roberts, Dorothy. *Killing the Black Body: Race, Reproduction, and the Meaning of Liberty.* New York: Vintage, 1998.

Robinson, Cedric. *Black Marxism: The Making of the Black Radical Tradition.* Chapel Hill and London: The University of North Carolina Press, 2000.

Rosen, Ruth. *Lost Sisterhood: Prostitution in America, 1900–1918.* Baltimore: Johns Hopkins University Press, 1983.

Rubin, Gayle. *Deviations.* Durham: Duke University Press, 2011.

Shah, Courtney Q. *Sex Ed, Segregated: The Quest for Sexual Knowledge in Progressive-Era America.* Rochester: University of Rochester Press, 2015.

Sharpe, Christina. *In the Wake: On Blackness and Being.* Durham: Duke University Press, 2016.

Shiffman, Jeremy, Michael Kunnuji, Yusra Ribhi Shawar, and Rachel Sullivan Robinson. "International norms and the politics of sexuality education in Nigeria."

Globalization and Health 14, no. 63 (2018). From https://globalizationandhealth.bio medcentral.com/articles/10.1186/s12992-018-0377-2.

Smith, Andrea. "Heteropatriarchy and the Three Pillars of White Supremacy: Rethinking Women of Color Organizing." In *Color of Violence: The INCITE! Anthology*, edited by INCITE! Women of Color Against Violence, 66–73. Boston: South End Press, 2006.

Smith, Sara, Pavithra Vasudevan, Carlos Serrano, and Banu Gökarıksel. "Breaking Families: Whiteness, State Violence, and the Alienable Rights of Kin." *Political Geography* 72 (2019): 144–6.

Smith, Andrea. "Queer Theory and Native Studies: The Heteronormativity of Settler Colonialism." *GLQ: A Journal of Lesbian and Gay Studies* 16, nos. 1–2 (2010): 42–68.

Smolak, Alex. "White Slavery, Whorehouse Riots, Venereal Disease, and Saving Women: Historical Context of Prostitution Interventions and Harm Reduction in New York City during the Progressive Era." *Social Work in Public Health* 28 (2013): 496–508.

Somerville, Siobhan. *Queering the Color Line: Race and the Invention of Homosexuality in American Culture*. Durham and London: Duke University Press, 2000.

Stallings, L. H. *Funk the Erotic*. Urbana, Chicago, and Springfield: University of Illinois Press, 2015.

"State by State Decisions: The Personal Responsibility Education Program and Title V Abstinence-Only Program." Sexuality Information and Education Council of the United States. Accessed March 15, 2011. http://www.siecus.org/index.cfm?fuseaction=Page .ViewPage&PageID=1272.

Swendiman, Kathleen. "Administration of New Abstinence Education Program Under P.L. 104–193." *Congressional Research Service*. March 6, 1997.

Terry, Jennifer. *An American Obsession: Science, Medicine, and Homosexuality in Modern Society*. Chicago: University of Chicago Press, 1999.

Tompkins, Kyla Wazana. "Intersections of Race, Gender, and Sexuality: Queer of Color Critique." In *The Cambridge Companion to American Gay and Lesbian Literature*, edited by S. Herring, 173–89. Cambridge: Cambridge University Press, 2015.

Transgender Europe. "Trans Day of Visibility Press Release: Over 2,000 trans People Killed in the Last 8 years," March 30, 2016. https://tgeu.org/transgender-day-of-visibility-2016-trans-murder-monitoring-update/.

UNESCO. "UN urges Comprehensive Approach to Sexuality Education," October 01, 2018. https://unesdoc.unesco.org/ark:/48223/pf0000260770.

Ungar, Mark. "State Violence and Lesbian, Gay, Bisexual and Transgender (lgbt) Rights." *New Political Science* 22, no. 1 (2000): 61–75.

U.S. House of Representatives. Committee on Energy and Commerce. *Extension of Funding for Abstinence Education*. Washington: Government Printing Office, 2002.

U.S Public Health Service Treasury Department. "Healthy Happy Womanhood: A Pamphlet for Girls and Young Women." Washington: Government Printing Office, 1920.

U.S. Senate. Committee Print of the Senate Special Committee. 98th Congress. 2nd Session. No. 98–496. *The Adolescent Family Life Act*. Washington: Government Printing Office, 1984.

U.S. Senate. Committee Print of the Senate Special Committee. 111th Congress. 2nd Session. *Patient Protection and Affordable Care Act*. Washington: Government Printing Office.

U.S. Senate. Committee Print of the Senate Special Committee. *Legislative History of the Omnibus Budget Reconciliation Act of 1981*, August 13, 1981.

U.S. Senate. Committee Print of the Senate Special Committee. *Social Security Act*. Accessed April 27, 2014. http://www.ssa.gov/OP_Home/ssact/title05/0510.htm.

Vance, Carole. "Innocence and Experience: Melodramatic Narratives of Sex Trafficking and Their Consequences for Law and Policy." *History of the Present* 2, no. 2 (Fall 2012): 200–18.

Weeks, Kathi. *The Problem with Work*. Durham and London: Duke University Press, 2011.

Williams, Ros. "Postcolonial Discourses and 'Sex Tourism.'" Accessed June 2020. https://www.e-ir.info/2011/08/15/postcolonial-discourses-and-sex-tourism/, 2.

Wilson, Woodrow. "Special Statement." Introduction to *Keeping Our Fighters Fit: For War and After*. Edward Frank Allen. New York: The Century Co, 1918.

Wonders, Nancy A. and Raymond Michalowski. "Bodies, Borders, and Sex Tourism in a Globalized World: A Tale of Two Cities – Amsterdam and Havana." *Social Problems* 48, no. 4 Special Issue (November 2001): 545–71.

Wu, Sara. "Revised Chinese Law Sparks Debate on Sexuality Education." *Reuters*, October 25, 2020. https://www.reuters.com/article/china-society-education-sex/revised-chinese-law-sparks-debate-on-sexuality-education-idUSL4N2HG01X.

Wynter, Sylvia. "Afterword: 'Beyond Miranda's Meanings: Un/silencing the "Demonic Ground" of Caliban's "Woman."'" In *Out of the Kumbla: Caribbean Women and Literature*, edited by Carole Boyce Davies and Elaine Savory Fido, 355–72. Trenton: Africa World Press, Inc., 1990.

Yeon, Jung Yu. "The Moral Code of Chinese Sex Workers." *Sapiens*, 2017. https://www.sapiens.org/culture/china-sex-trade-moral-code/.

Yung, Judy. *Unbound Feed: A Social History of Chinese Women in San Francisco*. Berkeley: University of California Press, 1995.

Zimmerman, Jonathan. *Too Hot to Handle: A Global History of Sex Education*. Princeton: Princeton University Press, 2015.

Index

Aberrations in Black (Ferguson)   23
abstinence education
    definition of   61
    significance of   62–7
Abu Ghraib   102
Adolescent Family Life Act
    (AFLA)   57, 58–9
Adolescent Pregnancy Program   57
affect   8, 75, 78, 112, 114, 121–3
    dysphoric   127
    hope and   123
    resistance and   153 n.24
    stuplimity and   127
    utopia and   123
Affordable Care Act   63, 65
African American men   37
African women,
    hypersexualization of   50, 72
Ahmed, Sara   70, 73, 75, 76, 78, 113, 125, 134, 153 n.24
Alexander, M. Jacqui   102
Alien Contract Labor Law (1885)   41
Alimahomed-Wilson, Jake   90
Allen, Louisa   85
Alves, Damares   97
American Journal of Sociology   2
American Obsession, An (Terry)   35
American Social Hygiene Association   8
Angelou, Maya   45
anti-homophobia kits   97
anxiety and erasure   109
Archard, David   81
Aresu, Alessandra   95
art, as experience   14, 141 n.9
autonomy   20, 82
Azoulay, Audrey   94

Baker, Josephine   19
Berlant, Lauren   110, 153 n.24
Bernstein, Elizabeth   104–5, 142 n.19
Bialystok, Lauren   82, 83

Binti (Okorafor)   132
biopolitics   20, 86, 89, 92, 98, 106, 149 n.28
    creation and reproduction and   13
    erasures and
        reorientation and   12–16
    Foucault on   80
    rationality and   80
    significance of   12–13, 100
    violence and   101
Black female reproduction,
    significance of   43
Black mothers
    dehumanization of   43
    demonizing   60, 62
Blacks   16, 17, 31–2, 53
Black women   39
    exploitation of   32, 39, 42, 50–1
    female sexuality and   37, 43
    normalizing degradation of   26–7
    in prostitution   26–7, 29–30, 40
    racial segregation of   32
Blair, Cynthia   27, 29, 30, 32, 33, 51
Bloch, Ernst   123
bodies and spaces   74–5
Bolsonaro, Jair   97
bourgeois freedom   91
Brazil   93, 97–8
    sex work in   99–100
breaks   124
Britzman, Deborah   84
Brockenbrough, Ed   21
Bromfield, Nicole F.   39
Bush administration   62
Butler, Octavia   131

Cabezas, Amalia L.   142 n.19
Cameron-Lewis, Vanessa   85
Canada   145 n.110
capitalism   62, 116, 120
    colonialism and   52–6

Index

domestic sex education policy
    and   91, 93, 98, 99
global   90, 107–9
heterogeneity and   54–5
late   108
liberal   20
modern   21
prostitution and   55
sex work and   24
systemic interconnectedness
    within   101–4
transnational   127
violent straightening and   71, 79,
    84, 86, 87
Carmody, Moira   85
Carter, Julian   11
China   93
    eugenics in   95–6
    sex work in   98–9
Chinese Exclusion Act (1882)   40
Christian Right   83
citizen-subject   91–2
clandestine pedagogies   129
clandestine praxes   131–7
Clinton administration   61
Cohen, Cathy   16, 20
colonialism   21, 44, 48–56
    capitalism and   52–6
    domestic sex education policy
        and   91, 93, 103, 105–6
    epistemology and   71–2
    heteronormativity of   49–50, 71
    masculine nature of   26
    racial difference and   50
    settler   49, 51–2, 105
    sex work and   105–6
    violent straightening and   71–3,
        79, 86, 87
    Western   24
Commission on Training Camp Activities
    (CTCA)   3, 22, 36–8
community   1, 15–17, 65, 66, 117, 132
    colonial logics and   50, 55
    domestic sex education policy
        and   99, 110
    imagined   68, 69, 100
    origin problems and   22, 26,
        30, 32, 44
    violent straightening and   72,
        73, 84, 85

Community Based Abstinence Education
    (CBAE)   62–3
Competitive Abstinence Education
    program   63
Comstock Act (1873)   8–9
Condom Nation (Lord)   8
Consolidated Appropriations
    Act (2010)   62
contagion, logic of   11
Conversation, The (De Lisio and Silk)   99
Corngold, Josh   82
criminalization   9, 91, 102, 106
    of deviant bodies   51
    of female sexuality   9
    justification of   53
    of prostitution   34, 42
    of sex work   38, 89, 98, 105
    of sex workers   99
critical hope   126
cruel optimism   109–10
Cruising Utopia (Muñoz)   24, 125
Cumming, Hugh S.   23

Davis, Adrienne   50–1
decriminalization   106, 111
Deer, Sarah   44
dehumanization   43, 50, 70, 72, 73,
    75, 78, 91
De Lisio, Amanda   99
Deloria Jr., Vine   145 n.112
democracy, significance of   81–3, 89,
    91, 104, 117
dependency, language of   62
desire
    colonial logics and   49, 50, 52, 53, 56
    domestic sex education policy
        and   91, 92, 98, 108–10
    imagination and alternatives
        and   112, 113, 115, 123–6, 129
    origin problems and   32, 39, 41
    significance of   6, 7, 9, 10, 13, 17, 58,
        67, 133, 134, 137
    violent straightening and   82,
        84, 85, 87
deviancy   16, 51, 54, 76, 77, 142
    domestic sex education policy
        and   104, 106, 108
    of female sexuality   57, 61
    idea of   35, 63, 66
    sexual   8, 13, 35, 48, 56, 62

deviant bodies, criminalization of   51
Dewey, John   141 n.39
district economies   28
domestic sex education
    policy, international
        implications of   89–90
    global points of exchange and   92
    policy exchanges   92–101
    sex work industry   104–7
    systemic interconnectedness
        within global capitalist
        economy   101–4
    illusive erasure and lessons
        and   107–10
    state violence and   90–2
Duggan, Lisa   125

Eagleton, Terry   126
educated hope   125–6, 154 n.40
Elliot, Missy   136
epistemology   12, 14, 15, 21, 109
    colonialism and   71–2
    depersonalization of   71
    imagination and alternatives
        and   113, 115, 118, 121, 123
    violent straightening
        and   70–2, 79, 87
erasure   51, 53, 68, 69–72, 100, 107
    biopolitics and
        reorientation and   12–16
    experiences, of sex workers   100
    extended, and contemporary
        control   56–61
        abstinence education   61–7
    illusive, and lessons   107–10
    of Native women   44, 45, 50, 72
    Queer of Color critiques and   20
ethnocentrism   55, 71
eugenics   10, 34
    in China   95–6
    racial mixing and   52
    settler colonialism and   51
    sterilization and   35

"family-first" narrative   103
felt intuition   121
female reproductive practices   56
    nonnormative   57
female sexuality   56, 84, 98, 140 n.17
    deviant   57, 61

    economic well-being and   58
    origin problems and   28, 31,
        33, 37, 38
    policing of   56
    public hygiene and   9–10
    as racialized   37
    stigmatization of   34
    White slavery and   43
Ferguson, Roderick   20, 23, 33, 39, 50,
    53, 70, 127
Fine, Michelle   85
Firmin, Michal   8, 11
Fosdick, Raymond   2, 3, 22, 36, 38, 73
FOSTA-SESTA acts   107
Foucault, Michel   7, 12, 19, 79, 80,
    142 n.22, 149 n.28
Freedom with Violence (Reddy)   91
Freire, Paulo   78
Freud, Sigmund   10
Funk the Erotic (Stallings)   23

Gather Together in My Name
    (Angelou)   45
Gilbert, Jen   84
Giroux, Henry   78, 119, 120
Goldman, Emma   108
Gonzolez, Janet   136
governmentality   33, 79
Greene, Maxine   78, 119, 120
Grouchy, Jillian   106
Gruenberg, Benjamin C.   22–3
Gutmann, Amy   81, 82

Hall, G. Stanley   10
Hall, Stuart   49
happiness   1, 3–4, 23, 106
    imagination and alternatives
        and   124, 125, 127, 128
    violent straightening and   76, 77, 79
Harney, Stefano   114, 128, 129,
    135, 137
Harper, Phillip Brian   121
Hayes, Carmen   69
"Healthy Happy Womanhood"
    pamphlet   3–4, 6
heterogeneity   54–5
heteronormativity   22, 45, 51, 103
    of colonialism   49–50, 71
    compulsory heterosexuality and   75
    marriage and   5–6

heteropatriarchy 33, 48, 71. *See also* patriarchy
heterosexuality 1, 20, 55, 83, 106
  compulsory 50, 75
High Schools and Sex Education 23
Hine, Darlene Clark 11, 42
homonationalism 101, 102
hope
  affective dimension of 123
  critical 126
  educated 125-6
  happiness and 124-5
  utopian demands and 124
Huber, Valarie 8, 11
human, concept of 73, 78, 87
  rationality and 79
humanization 12, 78, 80, 126
hypersexualization, of African women 50, 72

imagination 13, 48, 111-12
  knowledge and 119
  radical 17, 118, 120-2, 129
  significance of 119
imaginative impossibilities 118-24
  utopian demands and 123-4
indigenous women
  erasure of 44, 45, 50, 72
  neglect of 44
industrialization 9, 27-30
institutionalized policies, critique of 113
intersectionality 20, 86-7
Irvine, Janice 65

Jackson, Zakiyyah Iman 136
Jefferson, Thomas 43
Jensen, Robin 11, 34, 36, 37, 40
Jim Crow laws, significance of 10, 31
Johnson, Marcia P. 47
Jordan, June 135
justice 106, 112

Kantor, Leslie 94
Keeping Our Fighters Fit (Allen) 22
Keire, Mara L. 28, 30-2, 36-9
Kelley, Robin G. D. 120-3, 154 n.40
Kempadoo, Kamala 106, 142 n.19
Kendall, Nancy 65, 85
kinship 44, 72
  colonial logics and 48, 50, 51, 53, 55

domestic sex education policy and 98, 101, 103, 109
Kirby, Douglas 94
knowledge 49, 71
  female 58
  imagination and 119
  legitimate 14
  power and 24
  Reddy on 117-18
Koopman, Colin 7

Le Guin, Ursula 136
Levinson, Bradley A. U. 116
liberal democratic theory 81-3
liberal subject/liberalism 20, 58, 91, 116, 120, 155 n.5
  violent straightening and 82, 85-6
liberation 21, 70, 84, 89
  imagination and alternatives and 111, 112, 115, 119
Li Hongyan 95
Lomawamia, K. Tsianina 145 n.112
Lord, Alexandra 8-10, 60
love and surrealism 121-2
Lugones, Maria 48
Lungones 71

McAvoy, Paula 82, 83
McClelland, Sarah I. 85
McDonald, CeCe 135
McKittrrick, Katherine 136
Mann Act (1910) 10, 34, 39, 40, 42
marginalization 20, 55, 99, 100, 114, 133, 134
  violent straightening and 71, 79, 85, 87
Maternal and Child Health Block Grant 57
Mayo, Cris 83, 84
Meiners, Erica 153 n.8, 155 n.5
Michalowski, Raymond 105
Miller-Young, Mireille 69, 135
modern/colonial gender system 48
moral panic 55, 61
Moran, Jeffery 8, 10
Morrow, Prince A. 2, 8, 10, 30, 73
Moten, Fred 114, 128, 129, 135, 137
Moynihan Report (1965) 60
Muñoz, José Esteban 24, 125, 126, 154 n.40

National Association for the
    Advancement of Colored People
    (NAACP)   31
nationalism   89
    significance of   107–8
National People's Congress Standing
    Committee (China)   95
naturalization   16, 24, 50, 54, 67, 71, 76
neoliberalism   16, 21, 87, 133
    domestic sex education policy
        and   90, 98, 101–2,
        106, 108, 109
    education and imagination and   120
    funding and   58, 59, 61, 62, 65, 66
    imagination and   111, 117
Ngai, Sianne   127, 128
Nietzsche, Friedrich   123
Nigeria   93, 96–7
    sex work in   99
Nigeria Sex Workers Association   99
non-reproductive practices   76
    labor and   56
nonviolent practices   17, 101, 111, 116,
    117, 123, 124
normalization   7, 10, 13, 16, 48, 115, 119
    colonial logics and   49–52, 54
    domestic sex education policy and   90,
        100, 101, 105
    origin problems and   26, 33, 34
    violent straightening and   69,
        71, 76, 86
normativity   5, 7, 12, 14, 20, 32,
    55, 153 n.24
    domestic sex education policy
        and   90, 93, 95, 100–2, 108
    imagination and alternatives
        and   112, 113, 115, 116,
        119, 126, 127
    violent straightening
        and   70, 74–5, 84
"nowhere", possibility of   121
nuclear family model   53–4

Obama administration   63
Okorafor, Nnedi   132
Omnibus Budget Reconciliation
    Act (1981)   57
orientation   74–6, 101, 125, 127
origin problems   19
    criminal be definition and   33–8

Queer of Color critiques and   20–5
vice and   25–33
White slavery and   38–46

"Pamphlet for Girls and
    Young Women"   3
Parable of the Sower (Butler)   131
patriarchy   21, 28, 71, 73, 91, 105.
    See also heteropatriarchy
    funding and   49, 56, 58
Pedagogy of the Oppressed (Freire)   78
Personal Responsibility Education
    Program (PREP)   63–5
pessimism   129
phenomenology   73
Pillow, Wanda   113
policies, significance of   112–17
    power and   117
    research and   114–15
    state-sponsored   115–16
policing   91
    domestic   90
    of female sexuality   31, 33, 56
    of racial boundaries   33
    of sex work   48
    of White slavery   40
policy-oriented research   114–15
political rationality   12, 80
    sex workers and   13
Povenelli, Elizabeth   155 n.5
problematization   7, 19, 20, 113
Progressive/Progressive era   6, 9, 10,
    11–12, 51, 57, 60, 101
    origin problems and   32–3, 39,
        40, 44, 45
prostitute   2. *See also* sex worker
    African American   27
    Chinese   40–2
    education's lack of concern for   23
    eugenics and   34
    as lacking agency   143 n.37
    significance of   140 n.21
    stigmatization of   36
prostitution
    Black women in   26–7
    capitalism and   55
    criminalization of   34
    fear of   35
    history, in America   28–9
    as means of survival   27

participation in   29–30
  privileging of   105
  rape and   26
  significance of   25–6
  slavery and   26, 27
  as threat to national security   36–7
  White slavery and   39–40, 42–3
Puar, Jasbir   101–2
public hygiene discourse   8–9
  and female sexuality   9–10

queerness   84–5, 125–7
Queer of Color critiques   20–1, 47–8
  on colonialism   48–9
  in educational discourses   21–2
  sex work and   23–5
Queer Theory   20–1
Quijano, Aníbal   49

racial difference   50
racial mixing   31, 52
racism   6, 10, 11, 16, 57
  domestic sex education policy
    and   90, 91, 98
  origin problems and   20, 26, 28, 32,
    37, 38, 41–4
  violent straightening and   71, 73,
    75, 86, 87
radical imagination   17, 118, 129
  Kelley on   120–1
  love and surrealism and   121
  utopian consideration and   122
rationality   49, 71–3, 113
  biopolitical   80
  human as concept and   79
  political   12, 13, 80
  of state   80
Reagan administration   56–7, 60–1
Reddy, Chandan   20, 91, 117–18
Red-Light Abatement Act (1913)   42
red-light districts   3, 29, 36
  race riots in   31
reproductive freedom   11
reproductive practices   4, 13, 43, 50,
    52, 96, 109
  discriminatory   11
  freedom   11
  labor and   53, 56
  nonnormative female   57
  socially   21

respectability   8, 23, 36, 37, 87
  of jobs   28–9, 32
  White male   31
Rivera, Sylvia   47
Roberts, Dorothy   11, 43, 44, 60, 62
Robinson, Cedric   52
Rosen, Ruth   25, 26, 32, 33, 34, 39, 45
Rousseff, Dilma   97
Rubin, Gayle   108

St. James, Margo   111
Sangers, Margaret   11
schooling/schools   5, 9, 10, 11, 15, 16, 65
  abstinence and   64
  domestic sex education policy
    and   90, 92, 97
  funding and   63
  imagination and alternatives
    and   112, 114, 118, 129
  Native children and   145 n.112
  origin problems and   23, 25, 33, 44
  public   60, 82, 85, 100, 123, 124, 134
  violent straightening
    and   77, 82–5, 87
segregation   5
  housing   33
  institutional   42
  racial   32, 43, 50, 51
  reputational   31
  and vice   30–1, 39
Selective Service Act (1917)   36
settler colonialism   49, 51
  White slavery and   52
sex, significance of   1, 9
Sex Ed, Segregated (Shah)   11
sex education. *See also individual entries*
comprehensive   6, 92–7, 100, 107, 117,
    128, 145 n.110
  critique of   15–16
  discourses about   7–8
  as federally funded project   7–10, 12,
    38, 47, 49–52, 55, 56, 60, 63, 134
  Progressive era and   11–12
  purpose of   7–11
  White slavery and gaps in
    history of   38–46
sex instinct   4
sexism   27, 28, 57, 71, 73, 90
sex tourism   105
  modern industry of   106, 108

sexual abuse   42
sexual deviancy   8, 35, 62
sexuality
    biopolitics and   12
    Britzman on   84
    female   9–10, 34, 37, 43, 56–8
    Foucault on   13
    neoliberal attitude toward   65
    PREP on   65
    racialized   50
Sexuality Information and Education
        Council of the United States
        (SIECUS)   96
Sexuality in School (Gilbert)   84
sexual labor   90, 104, 105
sexual normativity, demand for   108
sexual pedagogies   111, 123, 126
    turn toward   117–18
Sexual Risk Avoidance Education (SRAE)
        grants   66–7
sexual subjectification   70, 93
sexual subjectivity   90, 92, 93, 107, 108
sexual violence   44, 48
sex work
as alternative space   24
    in Brazil   99–100
    in China   98–9
    criminalization of   38, 89, 98, 105
    industry   104–7
    marginalization of   100
    and marriage compared   108
    morality and   56
    in Nigeria   99
    reimagining of   23–4
    sex and sexuality and   25
    straightening and   76
    White slavery and   43–6
sex workers   5. *See also* prostitute
    as good students   69
    as irrational   73
    marginalization of   100
    political rationality and   13
    significance of   14, 140 n.21
Sex Workers Outreach Project   1
Shah, Courtney Q.   11
Sharpe, Christina   128, 154 n.51
Siebers, Tobin   137
silencing
    of Native women   44–5
    of sex work   67–8

Silk, Michael   99
slavery   47, 48, 50, 142 n.24
    origin problems and   21, 26–7, 32
    violent straightening and   71, 72, 79
    White   10, 11, 35, 38–46
Smith, Andrea   44, 71, 72
social hygiene   2, 8, 32, 35, 58
Social Security Act   61
Somerville, Siobhon   50
spaces and bodies   74–5
Springfield riot (1908)   31
Stallings, L. H.   13, 23–4, 136, 141 n.39
state-sponsored policy   115–16
state violence   81, 89, 90–2, 104, 107, 121
    human limits and   77–80
    meaning and significance of   79–80
    privatization of   90
sterilization   34–5
stigmatization   86, 87
    of deviant female sexuality   57
    of female sexuality   34
    of Native women   44
    of promiscuity   60
straightening   73–7, 113. *See also* violent
        straightening
    bodies and spaces and   74–5
    compulsory heterosexuality and   75
    sex work and   76
strangeness   84–5
structured paternalism   82
stuplimity   127–8
subjectification   19, 91, 125
    national   107
    normative   90
    processes of   48, 70
    sexual   70, 93
surrealism and love   121–2
Sutton, Margaret   116
Sweden   94

Taste for Brown Sugar, A
        (Miller-Young)   69
Teaching Sex (Moran)   8
teenage pregnancy
    funds and programs to prevent   63–4
    jobs and   59
Terry, Jennifer   35, 60
Thaler, Mathias   152 n.2
Tigert, John J.   23
Tompkins, Kyla Wazana   21

Too Hot to Handle (Zimmerman) 10
trafficking 16, 25, 71, 100, 107, 144 n.81
   of Native women's bodies 44, 45
training camp activities 2–3

ugly feelings 127
Unbound Feet (Yung) 41
Undercommons, The (Harney and Moten) 128
UNESCO 93
Ungar, Mark 102, 104
US Bureau of Education 22
US Public Health Service 22
utopian demands, idea of 123–4, 126, 129
utopian imagination 122–3

value judgments 74
Vance, Carole 144 n.81
vice
   districting 30–2, 51
   Progressive era and 32–3
   prostitution and 25–30
   reform 34
   segregation and 30–1
   sex education 33–4
violence 6, 56, 66, 67, 134
   biopolitical 101
   biopolitics and erasure and 13, 15–17
   colonial 71
   community and 100
   dehumanization and 78
   domestic sex education policy and 91–4, 100–3, 105
   epistemological 79
   freedom with 91
   human and 79
   imagination and alternatives and 111, 113, 115–17, 120–2, 125–6, 128, 129
   institutionalized 35, 98
   intersectionality and 86–7
   liberal framework and 86
   meaning and significance of 75
   nonphysical 78
   origin problems and 19, 21, 22, 26
   racial 32
   sexual 44, 48
   silencing and 44
   state 77–81, 89, 90–2, 104, 107, 121
violent straightening and state function 69–70
   human limits and state violence and 77–80
   rationalizing of human and 70–3
   significance of 73–7

Walker, Kanyia 89
Walkowitz, Judith 142 n.19
"War on Drugs" 60
Weeks, Kathi 54, 62, 123, 124, 154 n.40
White slavery 10, 11, 35
   meaning and significance of 38–40
   Native women and 44–5
   as racialized and gendered 40–2
   settler colonialism and 52
   sex education history
      as story about 43–4
      through prostitution and 42–3
   sex work and 43–6
White supremacy 71, 75
Williams, Dana 90
Williams, Ros 105, 106
Wilson, Woodrow 22
Winstead, Teresa 116
womanhood, healthy and happy 3–4
women's bodies, for entertainment 28–9
Women and Performance (Duggan) 125
Wonders, Nancy A. 105
work ethic 52–4, 56
Wynter, Sylvia 78, 79

Yeon Jung Yu 99
Young, Ella Flagg 11
Yung, Judy 41, 42

Zamolodchikova, Katya 137
Zimmerman, Jonathan 10, 151 n.17

www.ingramcontent.com/pod-product-compliance
Lightning Source LLC
Chambersburg PA
CBHW061837300426
44115CB00013B/2425